# Unix by Example

# A Handbook for New Users

# Unix by Example

# A Handbook for New Users

# P.K.McBride

NEW·TECH

Newtech
An imprint of Butterworth-Heinemann Ltd
Linacre House, Jordan Hill, Oxford OX2 8DP

$\mathcal{R}$ A member of the Reed Elsevier plc group

OXFORD LONDON BOSTON
MUNICH NEW DELHI SINGAPORE SYDNEY
TOKYO TORONTO WELLINGTON

First published 1993
Reprinted 1994

NOTICE
The author and the publisher have used their best efforts to prepare this book, including the computer examples contained in it. The computer examples have been tested. The author and the publisher make no warranty, implicit or explicit, about the documentation. The author and the publisher will not be liable under any circumstances for any direct or indirect damages arising from any use, direct or indirect, of the documentation or computer examples contained in this book.

TRADEMARKS/REGISTERED TRADEMARKS
Computer hardware and software brand names and company names mentioned in this book are protected by their respective trademarks and are acknowledged.

**British Library Cataloguing in Publication Data**
A catalogue record for this book is available from the British Library.

**Library of Congress Cataloguing in Publication Data**
A catalogue record for this book is available from the Library of Congress.

ISBN 0 7506 0637 1

Typeset by the author.
Printed and bound in Great Britain.

# Contents

## Part 2. Extending Your Range

**The Shells** 91

# Introduction

Unix is a powerful, open, multi-user and multi-tasking operating system that can be run on any computer from a high-specification PC up to a mainframe. Unix-based machines can exchange data freely and be linked into networks of unrestricted size, and any computer - with suitable communications software - can link into a Unix system and make full use of its facilities. Until recently, Unix systems were largely confined to educational and research institutions, but they are gaining favour in the business world. Large organisations appreciate its capacity to break down the barriers between desktop PCs and central computer systems, irrespective of the hardware. Smaller firms like the openness and expandability. In today's market, a Unix system based on a high-specification PC, and serving half a dozen users, can be set up for around £10,000 - but such a system can be expanded indefinitely if the need arose.

The bad news is that Unix was devised by programmers, for programmers, and compact power, not user-friendliness, was their prime aim. As a result, commands are terse, options legion, feedback sparse, and the potential for confusion high. Where a novice DOS user may take only a few hours to acquire sufficient understanding and confidence to be able to run applications and handle files, a new Unix user is likely to take days - and could still be making fundamental errors after months!

This handbook is intended for students and new business users. It aims to teach concepts and the use of commands by worked practical examples. It is based on the assumptions that, at first, you will only want enough to get by. Once into the system, there will be times when you want to explore different aspects in more depth. The structure of the handbook is a direct reflection of this approach.

The first part gives an overview of the Unix system - of files, directories and multiple users; an introduction to the key commands, with a minimum of options; and examples of typical working sessions. The text and examples are sequenced to create a foundation of basic understanding.

The second part is sub-divided by function, each section covering one or more related concepts or commands. The examples here build upwards from the foundations laid previously, but each is largely self-contained, so that the reader may pursue lines of interest independently.

The last part is a quick reference guide to the essential commands, giving for each a brief description of its purpose, major options and related commands.

Unix is not called that because it is either unique or unitary - it is neither. (Legend has it that it was so named because it was an emasculated version of an earlier operating system.) It was originally developed by AT & T, but over the years many academic institutions and computer corporations have contributed to its development. Unfortunately, not all the advances have been in the same direction, but two dominant versions have emerged - the official AT&T Unix System V, and the University of California Berkeley Unix. A recognition that compatibility rather than competition is the key to commercial success has encouraged increasing cooperation over the last few years, and installations nowadays are either Unix System V or a hybrid system that combines this with Berkeley Unix.For the practical user, the differences between varieties are not that significant - most of the same commands are there and they mostly work in the same way. So, even though the focus in 'Unix by Example' in on System V, much of what is said is equally applicable to any Unix system. While working on this book, I have been using SCO Unix on an Altos machine, and Coherent, a Unix look-alike from Mark Williams Company, on a DAN 486 PC.

Thanks to Tony Millard, who first introduced me to Unix, and to Colin Williams, for his help and tolerance.

P.K.McBride
December 1992

# Part 1

# Enough to Get By ...

# Chapter1

# You and Unix

In this chapter, you'll learn what we mean by 'Unix', and take a tour round a typical Unix computer system - from the outside and the inside. At this stage it is theory only, but in the next chapter you'll meet the commands that will get you into your own system. If you prefer to get 'hands-on' immediately, jump straight to Chapter 2 and come back to fill in the theoretical background later.

The first few pages are intended for those readers who are not only new to Unix, but new to computers. If you are already familiar with DOS-based PCs or other similar systems, you may prefer to skip to the next section.

## Computers and Operating Systems

Every computer system has three main components - the hardware, software and operating system.

It's **hardware** if it hurts when you drop it on your fingers. At the heart of the system there's the computer itself - the box that contains the processing and memory chips and other bits of silicon wizardry; all around it are the peripheral devices - the monitors, keyboards, disk drives, tape streamers, printers, modems and mice.

**Software** is sometimes described as the petrol that drives the computer engine. I prefer to think of it as gin. You can see its containers, and you can see its effects, but the stuff itself is almost invisible. Strictly speaking, the word "software" should cover any type of computer program, but it is more commonly taken to mean application programs. These include the office automation tools - word-processors, spreadsheets, databases, and communications and networking packages. Less obviously, applications also include programming languages, or at least, the programming tools that make the languages usable.

An **Operating System** is a particular type of software. It is a set of programs that control the computer at the lowest level. This is where you will find the detailed instructions that manage the access to the chips and disk drives and monitors and all the other devices. Without an operating system to look after your files, allocate resources to users and handle all the other nitty-gritty chores, using a computer would be a horrendously complex job. The operating system also makes it possible for applications software to run on the hardware. When a word-processor wants to load a file off a disk, it doesn't need to concern itself with how the disk is organised, how far to spin it or where to put the reading head. All that can be left to the operating system to sort out.

Operating systems make life easier for the writers of applications software in another way too. They smooth out the variations between different types of hardware, allowing the same program to be run across a range of computers. The part of the operating system that handles the hardware is rewritten for each new machine, but the part that communicates with applications programs (and with users) remains the same.

Unix is an operating system - and more. The Unix package is build around a central core, or **kernel**, that controls the hardware and the allocation of resources to users. A **shell** program handles the interaction between you, the user, and the computer. Amongst other things, it interprets your commands, and runs other programs for you. There is then a huge set of **commands** and **utility programs** offering a vast range of facilities - file-handling, directory management, file processing, text editing, messaging and electronic mailing, calendar and calculator, and more. The composition of this set varies between installations, though many of the utilities are common to all, and nowadays the set is huge. While the DOS operating system for PCs while fit on a single disk and can be documented in one moderately sized book, the Unix software typically runs to over 40 Megabytes and a dozen fat volumes of documentation.

# A Unix Computer System

## The Central Processor

The typical Unix system consists of dozens - possibly hundreds - of terminals connected to a single computer. The nature of this machine is largely irrelevant to most users. It can vary from a mainframe or minicomputer down to a high-power microcomputer. All that is necessary is that it should have sufficient processing power, memory and disk storage capacity to meet the needs of its users. Sometimes the computer will be *multi-tasking* - i.e. capable of doing several jobs at the same time. More commonly, it will run on a *time-share* basis. The central processor will spend a fraction of a second on a job for one user, then put it on hold - stashing it into memory - turn to the next job for a moment, then move on again. Though infinitely faster, it is not unlike a waiter in a restaurant, looking after a dozen tables. No diner has his undivided attention, but he is not missed as long as he is there when he is wanted. The computer may only be working on your job for a thousandth of a second at a time, but it will do so dozens of times a second - and that's faster than you can type!

On a good system, you shouldn't be aware of the fact that the computer is shared. It should be as responsive as a stand-alone desktop PC would be. This isn't always the case. If a system is getting close to its design limits, with too many users running demanding programs, or simply too many users altogether, then you may well become aware of the time-sharing aspect as the system slows down.

## Terminals and Peripheral Devices

On most Unix systems, the terminals are usually dumb, consisting of a keyboard and a monitor, but with neither processing power nor memory storage of their own. In some installations you will find intelligent terminals or workstations or even PCs connected into the Unix system. These are capable of doing some, or all of their own data processing. Increasingly, you will find monitors with full-colour, high-resolution graphics screen, but dumb terminals with simple text-only monitors are still the norm. They are quite adequate for the text and data processing that makes up so much of computing, and they are far cheaper.

There will always be at least one printer connected into the system, and there will usually be more - to cope with both the volume and the variety of the work. High-speed printers are needed to churn out program listings and database reports for internal reference; while for those jobs that must have a more polished finish, there will be slower, high-quality machines. Printers are normally connected to the system, not to an individual terminal. This means that you can print from anywhere on the system, and so, of course, can all the other users. To prevent clashes over access, all printing is done via the central computer. When a file is sent for printing, it joins a queue somewhere on a hard disk and is passed on to the printer when its turn comes. If you have worked in the past with PCs or other stand-alone computers, you will have to get used to waiting for your printouts.

Among the other peripherals devices you will almost certainly find a tape streamer, used to make backup copies of the data on the hard disks. As an ordinary user you wouldn't be expected to have do anything with this - backups are the responsibility of the system administrator. It's just reassuring to know that it is there, so that if you do erase files off the hard disks by mistake, you can get them back again.

## Your Place in the System

### Authorised Users

A key difference between any multi-user system and a stand-alone personal computer is in the control of access. With a PC, anyone who can sit at the keyboard and start up the machine, has full access to the hardware and any data stored on it. (Keys and passwords may restrict the initial access, but once past those hurdles, the computer is all yours.) A multi-user system is shared, and must be shared safely. That means that users must have their own places in which to keep data safe from accidental - or malicious - corruption by others. You can't just let anyone in, and even those who are allowed into the system, cannot be given free access to do what they want, wherever they like.

To become an authorised user of the system, you must be allocated a place to store your data and given a user name and a password. (You may be given an initial password and, as you will see later, you can change it at any time.) Armed with these, you can sit down at a terminal - any terminal - and get access to the computer (**login** in the jargon) by typing your name and password. We'll return to the details of this in the next chapter. At this point, the questions are, "When you've got access, where exactly are you, and what can you do there?"

## The Home Directory

Where you are, in terms of the system, is in your Home directory. This is the place on the hard disk where you will save any files that you create. And at this point, we should stop and look at hard disks and directory structures - and indeed, at the very concepts of files and directories.

## Files

A file is an organised body of information stored on a computer disk or tape, and identified by name. It may be an executable program, or a data file produced by an applications program. Its size may be anything from a few bytes (characters) to hundreds of Kilobytes (1K = 1024 bytes). In writing this book, for example, I am making use of a set of program files that together form the word-processing software, and creating a dozen or so data files, each containing a few chapters of text.

## Directories

Even the humblest hard disk has a huge amount of storage capacity. The 20Mb (Megabyte) disks found on entry-level PCs can store over 20 million characters. That's about 3 million words, or 30 books of this size. The hard disk capacity of a typical Unix system is 500Mb or more - the equivalent of several shelves full of books! Clearly, this must be organised in some way if you are ever to find any data in such a mass.

The solution is to sub-divide the storage space into directories, each one of which can have its own sub-divisions, and with each directory storing those files that belong to a particular user, or that relate to a particular

17

topic. In traditional filing terms, the hard disk is the equivalent of the room in which files are kept; the first level of directories are the cabinets, the second level are the drawers, the third are the hanging pockets. The sub-division can go further if necessary, with several folders kept in one pocket, and some folders containing batches of papers separated by divider cards. The analogy is slightly misleading as it implies that each directory is allocated a fixed amount of space, and that the process of division has to stop at some point. Neither is the case. In theory, a Unix directory can stretch to accommodate any number of files, and the sub-division can go on indefinitely. In practice, the hard disk sets an overall limit on the storage capacity, and a good system administrator will keep an eye on the amount of space that each user occupies. The sub-division also comes to an end once users decide that they have enough places to store different things - at least for the time being.

The Unix directory structure is usually represented as a tree - drawn upside down. It is not a fixed structure - every organisation will develop its own - but the overall shape and certain features are common to all.

**Figure 1.1**

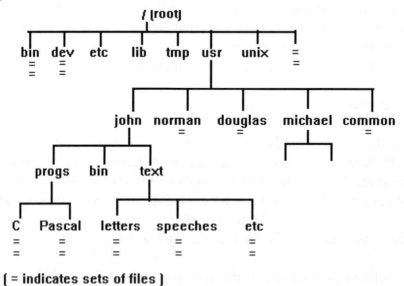

[ = indicates sets of files ]

The top of the tree is identified by a single forward slash (/), and called **root**. At the first level of divisions - the filing cabinets - you will find directories called 'bin', 'tmp', 'lib', 'etc', 'usr' plus others that are specific to your installation. There will also be a number of loose files up there, for they do not have to be stored in directories. A key one here is the 'unix' file, which contains the core of the operating system.

Those standard directories serve the same purposes on all Unix systems. Their names are too terse to be really meaningful, but they may help to remind you of their contents. As an ordinary user, you are unlikely to have much to do with what's going on up there, but it is useful to have an overview of the system. Some of these directories are sub-divided, others have a single mass of files.

**bin** - binary files, i.e. executable programs. These provide the main command set and file management utilities;
**dev** - devices - every terminal and other peripheral is linked to the system through a file in the dev directory;
**tmp** - the temporary files created by some programs;
**lib** - libraries of routines for some languages;
**etc** - files and directories for the system administrator's use;
**usr** - mainly applications, languages and users' directories.

We'll follow the division process further down 'usr', partly as an example of the structure, but mainly because your own directory is probably lurking somewhere in there. On a small business system, there may be no more than half a dozen or so directories - one for each user, and a few for shared files. In the example, the directories are 'john', 'norman', 'douglas', 'michael' and 'common'. What happens at the next level down depends upon the user. Some users like to subdivide their areas into several levels of directories; others will stick all their files into the one place. As with a paper filing system, it depends upon the number and variety of files, and on personal attitudes to organisation.

**Paths**

If you look closely at Figure 1.1, you will notice that the names of the directories are not unique. There are two named 'bin' and another two named 'etc'. This does not cause any problems. A directory is uniquely identified by its path. This tracks the sequence of directories from the root (/). Thus, the john's bin directory has a full path-name of '/usr/john/bin', while the other bin at the top of the system is properly called '/bin'. Likewise, the two etc's are '/etc' and '/usr/john/text/etc'. Notice that the forward slash (/) is used both to identify the root level, and as a divider between names.

In practice, you only need to give the full path if you are elsewhere in the system. At any given point, you can identify the directories immediately below you by typing their short names. When John is in his Home directory, '/usr/john', he can identify his 'bin' directory by a simple 'bin'. Similarly, you can identify any that branch off further down the same part of the tree by giving the remainder of the path. So, from '/usr/john', the etc directory would be called 'text/etc'.

But enough of theory, the best way to get to grips with directory structures and paths is to explore your own system, so let's get hands-on. In the many examples in the rest of the book, the following conventions will be used:

---

**Key to Examples**

| | |
|---|---|
| login | Already displayed on the screen. |
| **cd ..** | You type in exactly as given. |
| *filename* | You type and supply the actual name. |
| {comment} | Don't type this, it's my comment to you. |
| [Return] | Press the Return or Enter key. |
| [a] | Press the key to get the lower case letter. |
| [Shift][A] | Hold [Shift] and press to get the upper case letter. |
| [Ctrl]-[D] | Hold down the Control key and press the letter. |
| [Esc] | Press the [Escape] key - upper left corner. |
| [Backspace] | Sometimes marked [<-Del] or [<-]. |

---

## The Terminal

Terminals differ, but what follows should apply to most that are in use in Unix systems at the present.

### Reading the Screen

Most of the time when you working with Unix, the screen is simply a means of keeping a record of your recent interaction with the system. It will show the commands that you have entered, and the responses that the central computer has sent back to your terminal. Each new line that you type, or Unix sends back, will appear at the bottom of the screen, and earlier ones will scroll off the top. It is not an interactive display. This is an important point, often misunderstood by those who have used PCs and home computers. You cannot go back up the screen to edit what's written there, and you certainly can't recover those lines that have scrolled off the top.

The only part of the screen that you can edit is the line containing the prompt. Even then you are not really editing the screen itself. When you type in a command line, it is stored initially in a **buffer** (a small block of memory). When you press [Return], the command is passed from the buffer to the main computer, but until you do that, you can edit the buffer's contents. Which brings us to the keyboard.

### Using the Keyboard

Whenever you are in the Unix shell - i.e. giving commands - and in most of the utility programs, the same rules apply to the way that the keyboard works.

### Unix is case-sensitive

Lower case and upper case characters are different. 'fred', 'Fred' and 'FRED' are three different names. Unix commands, program names and most user names and written in lower case, so make sure your [Caps Lock] key is off. Hold down [Shift] and press a letter if you ever need an upper case character.

21

## Press [Return]
Press the [Return] or [Enter] key after you have typed in a command. Only then will the system take any notice of you.

## Spaces Matter
Whenever you type an option code or a filename after a command, you must leave a space.

## Correcting Errors
If you spot an error while typing in a line, you can correct it by pressing (Backspace). This deletes the last character - though the screen display may be misleading. On some systems, the cursor moves left but the character remains visible. This can be confusing. If you have Backspaced a character, it has been removed from the command line, even though you may still be able to see it. With some older systems, instead of deleting a character from the screen, the backspace adds a new one - usually #. For example, trying to give the command **date**, you mistype 'y' for 't', delete it then carry on. The resulting - correct - command line would appear to be 'day#te'.

## Mangled Lines
As both you and the system can write to the screen at the same time, the two can sometimes get intermixed and leave you with a garbled command line. Abandon it.

## Abandon Line!
It is often quicker to abandon a command line and start again from scratch, than to correct it. You can abandon a line by typing [@], or [Del] or [Ctrl]-[U]. Alternatively, just press [Return]. The system will try to interpret your command, fail and come back with an **Unknown command**, or similar, message. There is an outside chance that in mistyping one command you will have given a different one. It's unlikely but just in case ...

## Escaping from Programs
If you have set a program running by accident, or are stuck in one - both of which can happen even to experienced users - you can generally escape by pressing [Del] or [Ctrl]-[D]. One or other will stop most programs.

# Chapter 2

# An Hour with Unix

In this chapter you will get onto the system and use a few of the core commands. You will work your way around part of it, to see what's there and where you fit in, find out a bit about other users and about your shell. As Unix installations do vary somewhat, it is possible that some commands may have slightly different effects on your system. Don't worry about that at this stage. The reasons for the variations will become clearer later when we look at commands in more detail.

Before you can go any further, you'll need a terminal, and you must know your user name and password, if one has been allocated to you. Here, as always, if you have a problem with your system, consult your supervisor, lecturer or system administrator.

## Logging In

You should be looking at the login screen. This will normally carry the organisation's name and a message or greeting, and at the bottom there will be the login prompt. If you can't see this, check that the terminal is switched on, then try pressing [Return] a couple of times. This should make the system rewrite the screen.

Type in your user name, [Return] then - if required - type in your password. The characters will not be displayed on the screen, which makes for good security but frequent errors!

**login:** *username*
**password:** *your password*

If you make a mistake typing the password, it is probably not worth trying to correct it. Just press [Return], wait for the **Wrong password** message and try again.

After a successful login, you'll probably see a message from the system administrator. This is his chance to let users know what's going on.

> The system will be closing down at 4 o'clock today for the installation of additional memory. You should see an improvement in speed tomorrow.

You may also get a message telling you that you have mail. You should ignore it for the time being, but if you have a desperate urge to read it or to find out more about the electronic mail system, turn to Chapter 7.

## The Prompt

Beneath the message, you should see either a dollar ($) or percentage (%) sign. This is the prompt. (Yours may be something entirely different! Unix is highly adaptable and one its features that is very easy to change is the style of prompt. Your system manager may have decided to replace the single character with something more informative. Look and see what's there, then think of this whenever you see the dollar sign in the later examples.)

Whatever its style, the prompt shows that Unix is running a shell program for you, and that the shell is waiting to carry out your commands. Next to the prompt there will be an underline or a solid block, which will usually be flashing. This is the cursor. This is where text will appear when you type or when the system sends information back to you.

You must remember that you cannot normally edit the screen. That is, you cannot move the cursor around the screen and retype something. Well, it's physically possible on some systems, but it won't do any good. Unix normally works one line at a time. You type a command on the current line; if Unix sends something back in response to that command, it will appear on the following lines. The prompt and cursor then reappear on the next new line - which is then the current line. When the screen is full, the display will scroll up as new text is written at the bottom. Once lines have disappeared off the top of the screen, you cannot get them back except by redoing whatever it was that displayed them in the first place.

## Exploring Directories

We are going to use three commands here: **ls,** which lists the contents of a directory; **pwd**, which gives the path to the working directory, i.e. where you are; and **cd** to change from one directory to another.

**ls** See what's in your directory:

```
$ ls
$
```

You will probably see nothing at all - not even a message to say that the directory is empty, or even that it has run the command successfully. You will only get feedback when have specifically asked for it, or when you make an error.

**pwd** Find out where you are in the system:

```
$ pwd
/usr/staff/mac
```

That's what I see when I run **pwd**. What's your path? It will almost certainly start with '/usr', and immediately before your user name will be the name of the group of which you are a member. We'll climb back up the tree and see who else is in the group.

**cd** Change Directory

```
$ cd ..   { space after the cd }
$
```

A **..** (double dot) after the change directory command says "up one level". There's no visible effect, and no message, but that's Unix for you. It presumes that you knew what you were doing when you gave the command, and it has been performed successfully, so what is there to say?

25

Let's check where we are and find out what's there.

```
$ pwd
/usr/staff
$ ls
colin
mac
mike
nadia
tony
trisha
$
```

**pwd** simply confirms where we are - it doesn't do anything useful. **ls** lists the files and directories stored in the directory. In the example it lists the Home directories of the staff users. What do you see when you do it? Most of the names should be those of the directories of other members of your group, though there may be some files there as well.

N.B. In some systems, a simple **ls** will list the items in columns across the screen - on others you must use an option (see Chapter 4) to get this display.

Try to change to the directory of one of the other users. To do this, type **cd** followed by a user name from the list. You will almost certainly be greeted with a **Permission denied** message. You cannot enter other users' areas - without their express permission - any more than they can enter yours.

We'll explore directories further in the Chapter 4. Meanwhile, return to your Home directory with an unqualified **cd**. If you don't say where you want to go, the system assumes you mean home.

## Looking Around

### who Who's There?

You've seen who is in your group, but who else is logged onto the system at the moment. Find out by typing **who**.

```
$ who
root      console     Mar 27 11:50
root      tty02       Mar 27 14:09
fred      tty137      Mar 27 13:39
mac       tty147      Mar 27 14:53
nadia     tty152      Mar 27 13:47
steph     tty167      Mar 27 13:43
```

For each current user, this gives the name, the terminal number (the console is the one directly attached to the computer) and the date and time when the user logged in. And when you next have an identity crisis, try this:

```
$ who am i
mac       tty147      Mar 27 14:53
```

## date Finding the Date and Time

How does the system know when users log in? Along with most other types of computers, Unix systems have a combination clock and calendar. As long as the system administrator sets it correctly at first start-up (and adjusts it for Summer Time), it can always tell you the right time and date. If you ever want to know, just type:

```
$ date
Fri Mar 27 14:53:58 GMT 1992
```

## Which Shell?

When you type a command, you are not talking directly to the Unix operating system, nor does it report back directly to you. Instead, you are working within a **shell** program. This intercepts everything you type, checks to see that it is a meaningful command that it can perform, and either does the job or tells you why it can't. It has other roles as well. It is through the shell that you can control your working environment. The shell also contains its own programming language. None of this is particularly important at this stage, and a casual user need never bother much with most aspects of the shell. However, one thing is worth knowing at this stage. Which shell are you in?

Several different types of shell are found on Unix systems - the commonest being the Bourne shell and the C shell. They are very similar in many respects, and will interpret your commands in the same way, but there are some significant differences. The Bourne shell is probably the most widely used at present, and has the best programming capabilities. The C shell has a number of features that can make life easier for the user, but has a more limited programming language. A more recent alternative is the Korn shell, which combines the best of both. It is fully compatible with the Bourne shell, so that shell script programs written in either shell will work with the other, and it is as good as the C shell for interactive work.

To find out what type of shell you have, look first at the prompt. If it is a $, you are in a Bourne shell; a % indicates a C shell. If your prompt is neither of these, here's a second way of checking and one which will take us a little deeper into the system. Type:

```
$ ls -a            {space after the ls}
.    ..    .profile  { or .login and/or .cshrc }
```

Here we are setting an option for the **ls** command. **-a** tells it to list All files. Those with a name starting with a dot are omitted from the list produced by a simple **ls**. They are omitted because these are usually system files - not ones that you would generally want to change or delete. The first two in the list . (called 'dot') and .. ('dot dot') cannot be deleted. These are the directory itself (dot) and the link up to the next directory in the structure (dot dot). They are vitally important, but right now we are interested in the files that follow them.

If you are working within a Bourne shell, you will have a file called '.profile'. If yours is a C shell, with a % prompt, you will probably see '.login', and possibly a '.cshrc' file. (Neither is essential and some system managers set up their systems to run without them.) In either case there might also be a '.logout' file.

## Your Environment

The .login, .profile and .cshrc files are shell programs, which are run automatically when you log in and which set up your working environment. The most important aspect of this is probably the **PATH**, which determines where Unix should look for programs. Other environmental settings include the style of your prompt, the timezone and the nature of your terminal. The '.logout' file is executed at the end of your working session. Precisely what is in these files varies enormously. When the system administrator first creates your directory, standard files will be copied into it. As you will see later, you can edit these, to customise the system to your own needs. For the moment, if you want to see what is in these files, try this:

> $ **cat .profile**      {space after the command}
> ...
> % **cat .login**      {or **cat .cshrc**}
> .....

**cat** displays a text file on the screen. The name is derived from the word 'concatenate', which means join together and refers to another function of this same command. It is covered more fully in Chapter 12.

## **passwd** Changing your Password

You can change your password at any time - and should change it regularly if you want to keep your files secure. Different systems vary slightly in their rules on passwords, but in general passwords should:

have at least six characters, and can be longer, though only the first 8 characters count;
contain at least 2 letters and 1 number or symbol;
be different from the login name;
be at least three characters different from the old password.

To change the password, call up **passwd** and follow the instructions. When you type the new password it will not appear on screen, so you will be asked to retype it as a check.

> $ **passwd**
> New password:            {type carefully!}
> Retype new password:     {exactly the same again}

Next time you log in, use the new password. If you forget it, then all is not lost as the system administrator, or anyone else with **superuser** access, can let you in to set up a new password. (With superuser access you can do anything you like, for all files and directories are open to you. Knowledge of the root password, that grants this access, is generally a closely-guarded secret.)

## Logging Out

Our hour must be up by now - but if it isn't, and you would like to leave your mark on the system, why not create a few 'instant files'. (See next page.)

When you have finished your session with Unix, you must log out. This frees the terminal for other users and closes the access to your part of the system. Failure to log out will allow other users to get into your directory. On some systems you can log out with the single keystroke [Ctrl]-[D]. On others you exit by typing:

### $ **logout**

There might be a few seconds delay while the system thinks about it, but you can be certain that you are logged out when the login screen comes back into view.

# Instant Files

Unix allows you to redirect output to a file. That is, instead of a program or command producing a display on the screen, the text can be written to a file. If you use the technique with a **who** or an **ls** directory listing, you will have a copy of the output which you can read on screen later or print out for permanent reference. At this stage of your learning, you may find this a handy way to create files, which you can then work on when trying out the various file management commands.

Redirection is simple. At the end of the command line, just add the symbol '**>**' and the name that you want the file to be called. (Do **cd** first to make sure that you are back in your Home directory. If you try to create files while you are elsewhere in the system, you will probably be refused permission to do so.)

```
$ cd              { go home! }
$ who > wholist   { or whatever filename you like }
$ ls
wholist
```

Nothing will appear on the screen after the redirected command, but when you run **ls**, the file 'wholist' will be there in the listing. If you want to check what's in the file, use 'cat wholist' to display it on screen. Try the same technique to send the **date** output to a file.

```
$ date > datefile
$ cat datefile
Fri Oct 30 14:53:58 GMT 1992
```

31

# Chapter 3

# Editing Text with vi

It is possible that you may not need to read this chapter. **vi** is the most widely used of the Unix text editors, and is supplied as standard with almost all Unix systems, but there may be an alternative - and easier - editor in your installation. Do check with your supervisor or system administrator before going any further.

**vi** is so-called because it is a *visual* editor - text is displayed and edited on screen. Those of you familiar with word-processors, will probably see this as being the only way to create text, but when **vi** first appeared, on-screen editing was a novelty to Unix users. Its predecessor, **ed**, was a line-based editor. With this, to edit a line of text, you had to call it up by its line number. It did have some powerful editing facilities, and with practice, users could edit text very efficiently with **ed**. It is still supplied with most Unix packages and its command set is present within **vi**. Some of those commands are useful, and we will look at them later. There is far more to **vi** than most of us need. We'll stick to the core set.

## Write Mode and Edit Mode

You must understand from the start that vi has two distinct modes of operation - write and edit. When you are in **write mode** you can only write new text, and cannot alter what's already written - apart from using [Backspace] to erase characters in the current line. To delete, alter, move or otherwise edit existing text, you must go into edit mode.

In **edit mode**, the letter keys call up different functions - and lower case and upper case have different effects. To save confusion, keep the [Caps Lock] off when editing.

There are dozens of editing commands, but the few given below should be enough for the time being. Most are run from a single keypress, though two need a double click on the same key.

| Edit Keypress | Effect |
|---|---|
| [a] | Switch to Write mode, adding after cursor |
| [i] | Switch to Write mode, inserting before cursor |
| [o] | Switch to Write mode, opening a new line below |
| [x] | Delete character under cursor |
| [r] *char* | Replace character under cursor with new *char* |
| [d][d] | Delete whole line |
| [p] | Paste (deleted) line back into the text |
| [u] | Undo the last edit operation |
| [Z][Z] | Save and exit. (Note CAPITAL Zs) |
| [h] or ← | Left one character |
| [j] or ↑ | Up a line |
| [k] or ↓ | Down a line |
| [l] or → | Right one character |

To return from Write to Edit mode, press [Esc].

## Getting out of Trouble

Careful! Almost every key has a special function in Edit mode - some calling up fairly complex routines. If you get into difficulties, here are some possible solutions:

[u] undoes the last edit - i.e. whatever you have just deleted or inserted. The key sequence [:] [q] [!] will usually take you right out of vi and back to your shell. When you press [:], you should see a colon appear at the bottom of the screen. (This is where the **ed** commands are given.) The 'q!' - meaning 'Quit and Abandon the edit' - should also be displayed down there.

If you don't see this, it means you have called up one of the advanced editing routines, and you will have to get out of that before you can do anything else. Either [Return] or [Del] will generally cancel these routines.

If all else fails, ask your supervisor for help!

## Creating a New File

We are going to create a short file called 'fox', containing the sentence 'The quick brown fox jumps over the lazy dog.' (If nothing else, it will make you find every letter on the keyboard.) Try to follow this first example exactly as given, letter for letter - including the deliberate mistakes.

1) Call up the vi program and give a name for the file you are going to create:

**$ vi fox**
```
>
>
>
>
>
>
>
>
```
"fox" New File

2) The screen will clear, with the cursor sitting up in the top left corner. The >s down the left hand side indicate empty lines. At the bottom you will see a reminder of the filename. If it is not there, it means that you forgot to specify the name when you started vi, and you will have problems later when you try to exit. So, if you can't see the filename, exit now by pressing [:] [q] then start again.

3) Press [a] to switch into **Write** mode. Type:

**The quock_**

4) Stop! You have a mistype, and you've only just gone past it. Rub out back to the error by pressing [Backspace]. Now complete the sentence, with these errors and omissions. Press [Return] at the end of the line.

**The quick ffox jimps ocer the lazzy dog. [Return]**
      ^ ^                    ^ ^

5) Press [Esc] to return to **Edit** mode. Start by deleting the unwanted characters. Move the cursor, using the arrow keys or [h] [j] [k] [l], to the first 'f' of 'ffox'. Press [x] to delete it. Move on to a 'z' in 'lazzy', and press [x] again.

**The quick fox jimps ocer the lazy dog.**
           ^        ^

6) Now for the mistypes. Move the cursor to the 'i' in 'jimps'. Press [r], for single character replace, then the correct letter 'u'. Move on and use again to turn 'ocer' into 'over'.

**The quick_fox jumps over the lazy dog.**
          ^

7) One last edit. We missed out 'brown'. Move to the space after 'quick' and press [a]. This switches you back into Write mode. Type 'brown' (and a space), then press [Esc] to end writing. The old text will shuffle to the right to make room for your new addition.

**The quick brown fox jumps over the lazy dog.**
**[Z][Z]**

8) Done! Time to save and exit. Hold down [Shift] and press [z] twice. This will close down vi and take you back to the shell prompt. Give an **ls** command to list the files, and you should see 'fox'.

```
$ ls
fox
```

Right, now do it all again to fix what you have just learned. Call up vi and create another one-line text file. If you want to take another Cook's tour of the keyboard, you might like this more modern alternative to the old chestnut. 'My faxed joke won a pager on a cable TV quiz show.'

$vi fax

Take it away. Remember:

| | |
|---|---|
| [a] | to add new text; |
| [Backspace] | to erase mistakes in Write mode; |
| [Esc] | to get back to Edit; |
| [x] | to delete; |
| [r] | to replace when editing; |
| [Shift][Z][Z] | to save and exit. |

Once back at the shell prompt, check your directory, and you should find that it now contains two files.

```
$ ls
fox
fax
```

## Editing an Existing File

We are going to get the 'fox' file back into vi and add a few lines. This will bring a few more commands into play and demonstrate some key points about multi-line files. As before, please try to follow the example letter by letter.

1) Call up vi, giving it the name of the file to be edited:

**$ vi fox**

2) The screen will clear. At the top you will see your old text and at the bottom the status line will tell you that this is "fox" and that it has 1 line and 45 characters. The cursor will be at the top left, on the first character. Press [o] to open a new line below the current one and switch to Write mode. Add the text as shown, using [Backspace] to correct as you go along. Press [Return] at the end of each line, and [Esc] when you have done.

The quick brown fox jumps over the lazy dog.
**First new line**
**Line 2**
**The last line.**

3) Try to move over the text using [h][j][k][l] or the arrow keys. Notice that the cursor won't move into the blank area at the ends of lines. If you wanted to write something in this area, you would have to press [a] to add at the end of the line.

4) Move the cursor to the top line - anywhere along it - and press [d][d]. This will delete the line.

The quick brown fox jumps over the lazy dog.    { **[d][d]** }
First new line
Line 2
The last line.

5) The line is gone, but it is not forgotten. Deleted text is stored in a buffer (a block of temporary memory). To put it back into the text, move the cursor to the line above where you want it to go - in this case "The last line" and press [p].

First new line
Line 2
The last line.        { **[p]** }
**The quick brown fox jumps over the lazy dog.**

6) Save and exit by pressing [Z][Z].

To consolidate what you have learned so far, use vi to write a summary of the vi commands. You can then print it out for quick reference. Which brings us to ...

## Printing and Printer Control

In a multi-user system, users cannot send text directly for printing whenever they want to - a printer can only work on one item at a time. The Unix solution is to process files through a queue. When you send a file for printing, it goes first into temporary storage on the hard disk, and is then passed on to the printer when its turn comes round. We will come back to queue management in a moment. The important thing to realise at this point is that the queue is there, and that there will be a delay (of a few seconds or a few minutes) before your text hits the paper.

Before you try to do anything with the printer for the first time, check with your supervisor or system administrator. As long as you stick with files and directories inside the machine, all Unix systems are essentially the same, and there's little or nothing that the ordinary user can do that will create problems for anyone other users. Once you start interacting with external hardware, you run into variations and problems.

It is quite likely that your system has its own set of commands - custom-built shell scripts - to make printing simpler and safer. These will be two main problems that it aims solve. The first is to make sure that your file reaches the right printer. The is mainly a simplification, as it saves having to give the device identification, which may be necessary with a standard print command. The second will be to stop any non-printable files from reaching the printer. When I first started working with Unix, it was on a system that had no such trap. As a result, several times a week a student would accidentally send a compiled (machine code) file down to the printer, and the printer would go berserk. Each fit of madness would waste umpteen sheets of paper, and to restore sanity it was sometimes necessary to turn off the whole system - not just the printer! So, do check with your powers-that-be.

The standard command to print a file is **lp** and it must be accompanied by the name of the file, and possibly by the printer's identifier. Check with your supervisor before you go further.

```
$ lp filename          { name of file to print }
request id is pr1-5786 (1 file)    { or something similar }
```

The message "request id ..." lets you know that the file has been placed in the queue and will be printed - sometime. The ID identifies the file in the print queue.

If your file has not been printed by the time you get to the printer, and there's a lot of people hanging around waiting for theirs, and you don't really want to wait, then help is at hand. Go back to your terminal and check the queue.

## The Print Queue

The command **lpstat** tells you the status of the line printer. 'line' simply means that it is 'on-line' to your system, and is not a reference to the type. Used by itself, the command just tells you about your current print requests:

```
$ lpstat
pr1-6983          muggins          6625  Dec 18 11:31
```

To find out more about the queue, you must specify the -t option. This will tell you about all the printers and the files that are in the queue:

```
$ lpstat -t
scheduler is running
system default destination: pr2
device for pr2: /dev/tty032
device for pr1: /dev/tty137
pr2 accepting requests since Thu May 28 17:42:24 1992
pr1 accepting requests since Tue Dec  8 10:27:42 1992
pr2-6965          orc              6356  Dec 18 11:27
pr2-6970          swift            4084  Dec 18 11:28
pr1-6976          peony            3219  Dec 18 11:29
pr2-6982          swift            4084  Dec 18 11:30
pr2-6983          muggins          6625  Dec 18 11:31
pr2-6984          vampire          5570  Dec 18 11:32
```

And there are you, muggins, stuck almost at the end of the queue! You have got two choices. You can be patient, or you can cancel the print request, knock off for the day and  try again tomorrow.

To cancel a print-job, all you need to know is its ID. This is the one that was displayed when you first sent the file for printing. In case that is no longer visible on your screen, it is also displayed in the left hand column of the **lpstat** output. The command is a plain:

$ **cancel pr2-6983** { or whatever ID number }

NB. There's no point in trying to jump the queue by cancelling other people's print-jobs. You can only **cancel** your own.

# Filenames

Unix is fairly easy-going in its rules about filenames, though there are certain conventions. A filename is normally a single word, or a name and a suffix, separated by a dot (.) e.g.:

chapter1.txt, stock.c, chapter1.bak, mytext.

The **suffix** is used to identify the type of file, for the benefit of the user or of an application program. (It has no special meaning to Unix.) You might chose to label text files with a '.txt', and backup copies with a '.bak' suffix. Most language compilers insist that source files have special suffixes, such as .bas (Basic), .c (C), .pas (Pascal), .cbl (Cobol).

The **maximum length** of filenames varies between systems, but is typically 14 characters. These can be almost any characters, though some are best avoided. Use letters and digits only, and you won't go far wrong.

If you want to have **more than one word** in the filename, use the underscore (_) or dot (.) as a separator. Don't use spaces, as Unix treats spaces as marking the ends of words.

The symbols * ? [ ] - ( ) \ ' " ; : ! have special meanings and should be avoided. If you start a name with a dot, it will not normally be displayed by **ls**, which can be useful if you want to tuck a file out of the way.

Be consistent in your use of **upper** and **lower case**, as Unix treats them as being different. 'MYPROG' is not the same as 'myprog'.

**Make your filenames meaningful.** They should remind you instantly of the contents or purpose of the file. Keep them short if possible. Long names give more opportunities for typing errors.

| | |
|---|---|
| stock92.data | {good name for this year's stock records} |
| letter | {poor - O.K. by Unix, but meaningless} |
| john.memo | {could be more informative and....} |
| John.memo | { ... you'll confuse it with this one} |
| .hidden | {good if you want to keep it discrete} |

# Chapter 4

# Exploring Directories

In this chapter we'll explore a typical directory tree structure, find out what is kept in some key directories, then see how to create sub-directories to suit your filing needs.

Back in Chapter 1, you met the definitions of a file as an organised body of information stored on a disk, and a directory as a place on the disk where files can be stored. They remain good working definitions and probably the best way to think about them, but they don't tell the full story. In Unix, a directory is a file - albeit a special sort of file. The operating system sees a directory not as space on the disk, but an index to where files are stored. When you change directory, you are turning to a new place in the index.

In practice, you don't need to worry much about this distinction, but it does have a couple of important considerations. It means that the same rules apply to directory names as to filenames, and that directories and files are listed together when you type ls. It's not difficult to tell which is which, as you will see when we look at the **ls** options - but to do that properly, we need to find some directories with a bit of variety in them. So first, let's go exploring.

## The Directory Tree

Figure 4.1 is a simplified view of a typical structure - simplified by giving only the sub-divisions of one directory at each level. It is based on the system that I work with, and shows what I see as I move up and down the tree. It will be useful at this stage to draw a similar diagram for your own system. Apart from being a good exercise, it will produce a reference map for later use.

**Figure 4.1**

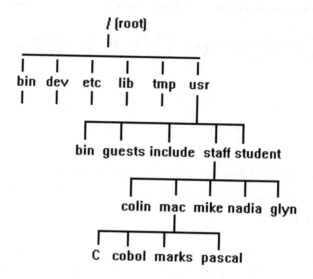

1) Start by making sure that you are in your own directory. Type **pwd** to get the path. If your user name is not the last item in the path name, you have strayed from home. Get back to your directory by typing **cd**.

2) You are going to move up a level, check the path and list the directory contents. The screen display should be something like this.

```
$ cd ..        { change to the directory above }
$ pwd          { path to working directory }
/usr/staff
$ ls           { list directory contents }
colin          { and yours will be different of course}
mac
mike
nadia
tony
$
```

3) Repeat that same sequence of commands - **cd .. pwd ls** - to work back up to the top of the tree, looking around you as you go.

```
$ cd ..  { change up}
$ pwd    { check the path}
/usr
$ ls     { list }
bin
include
staff
students
$ cd ..
$ pwd
/                  { the top of the tree }
$ ls
bin
dev
etc
lib
tmp
unix
usr
```

4) When the path is a single slash (/) you know you have reached the top. At that level, you should find the same core of directory contents in every Unix system. There will always be 'bin', 'dev', 'etc', 'lib', 'tmp' and 'usr' directories - and the unix program file. What's in these directories? Why not go and look? Some of them should be open for you to view.

5) To change into a directory that appears in the list, just type the name after **cd** - don't forget the space after the command word.

```
$ cd bin
$ ls
acctcom
aomlogin
ar
...
...
vax
who
write
```

There's an awful lot of stuff in the 'bin', isn't there! These are the main set of command and utility programs. If you are quick, you might spot **login**, **pwd** and **ls** as they shoot by. (You'll find out how to control these displays shortly.)

6) Spend a little time moving around the directories to get the feel of the structure. Use these **cd** options, changing directory names to suit your system:

| | |
|---|---|
| **cd ..** | up one level |
| **cd /** | leap to the root from anywhere |
| **cd /etc** | up to the root then down to etc |
| **cd dir1/dir2** | down through dir1 to dir2 |
| **cd ../..** | up two levels |
| **cd** | back to your Home directory |

You may find that some of your **cd** commands are not obeyed, in which case you should see an error message:

**Permission denied** shows that you attempted to change into one owned by another user, or into one that is closed to ordinary users.

**Not found** tells you that you have got the name (or path) wrong. On some systems, if you type a near-miss (the odd letter wrong), the system will try and guess what you meant.

```
$ cd bim     { ends in 'm' }
cd bin? y    { or 'n' if you didn't mean that one}
```

## ls - List Directory Contents

So far we have just used **ls** to list files and sub-directories. This gives a simple, names-only display. Sometimes, that is not enough - and sometimes it is too much. **ls**, like many other Unix commands, has several optional variations, each identified by a single letter. To invoke an option, write a dash and then the code letter after the command. e.g.

**ls -l**    {specifying the long directory listing}

Note that space after **ls**. Miss it out and the system won't know what you're talking about. Take care with cases. Some options are identified by capitals, others by lower case. **ls -L** is quite different from **ls -l**.

**ls** has some two dozen optional variations. Most of these can be safely ignored, but these five are worth knowing about.

## ls -l The Long List

Let's try the long list now and find out more about the way that files are stored. We need a directory with something in it, of course. The root will do nicely.

```
$ cd /    { go to the root}
$ ls -l   { long list }
total 495
drwxr-xr-x  2  bin   bin      1504  Apr 13 14:37 bin
-rw-r—r—   1  root  sys     19244  Apr 13 12:15 boot
drwxr-xr-x  4  root  sys      1424  Apr 13 13:13 dev
drwxr-xr-x  7  root  sys      1488  Apr 23 00:08 etc
drwxrwxrwx 3  bin   bin       384  Apr 13 13:48 lib
drwxr-xr-x  2  root  root     1024  Apr 13 13:13 lost+found
drwxrwxrwx 3  root  root       80  Apr 23 02:41 tmp
-rw-r—r—   1  root  sys    204975  Apr 13 12:15 unix
drwxr-xr-x 19  bin   bin       320  Apr 23 00:08 usr
```

Compact, coded information like this may be a bit forbidding at first glance, but it makes sense when you start to break it down. I'll head up the listing and work through the columns one at a time.

| Permissions | links | owner | group | size | date | time | name |
|---|---|---|---|---|---|---|---|
| drwxr-xr-x | 2 | bin | bin | 1504 | Apr 13 | 14:37 | bin |
| -rw-r—r— | 1 | root | sys | 19244 | Apr 13 | 12:15 | boot |

The first character indicates the type of file. 'd' stands for directory; '-' is a normal file. Elsewhere in the system, particularly in the '/dev' directory you will find 'b' which marks block storage media - the hard and floppy disks; and 'c' for character-based files, i.e. the terminals. (Yes, terminals are also files in Unix, but don't let that bother you.)

## Permissions

The permissions tell you who has what sort of access to the file. There are three sets, each of three characters. The first set are the permissions enjoyed by the owner (**user**) of the file, the second by other members of his **group**, and the last by all the **others** on the system.

```
user  group  others
rwx   r-x    r-x    .... bin
rw-   r—     r—     .... boot
```

The **access modes** are:
   **r** read - and display, copy and similar, but without changing it in any way;
   **w** write - and edit, rename and delete;
   **x** execute a program, or have full access to a directory.

In Chapter 6 you will see how to change permissions to make your files more secure.

## Links

The links figure is a bit technical. Essentially it tells you how many directories are linked to that file. Ordinary files will normally have only one link. Directories have at least 2 - one to themselves and one to the directory above. Anything higher than this indicates that the directory has sub-directories.

## Owner and Group

These should be obvious. If you find any in your directory that do not list you as the owner, then ask your system administrator to investigate!

## File Size

The size of a file is measured in bytes. Shortage of storage space can be a problem on multi-user systems. If it is on yours, then it's worth knowing which files could free up most space if removed.

## Date and Time

The date and time refer to when the file was last updated. When the system administrator is running the backup routine, the system will refer to this to pick out those files that have been changed since the time of the last backup.

## Other ls Options

### ls -C Column-wise List

This lists files, by name only, in columns - very useful where there are lots. Try it in the '/bin'.

```
$ cd /bin
$ ls -C
acctcom chown   du        kill    mail    pdp11  size u3b
aomlogincmp     dump      l       make    ps     sleep
u3b10
....
....
chgrp   diff    ipcrm   lx      od       sed    tty
chmod   dirname ipcs    m68k    passwd   sh     u370
```

### ls -F List with Filetype

This also lists in columns, but adds a file type indicator at the end. '*' marks executable programs, '/' a directory. The 'bin' isn't very interesting for this - they are all executable. Try your 'etc' directory:

```
$ cd /etc
$ ls -F
add.hd* ff*    layout*    mvdir*    swap*
admcrontab filesave*  layouts/   ncheck*   sys.start*
....
....
```

Your display is unlikely to be the same as this, but you should find that most are executable* programs, with a scatter of directories/ and (unmarked) data files.

## ls -a List All

This fourth option lists all files, including those starting with a dot, that are normally ignored. We met this before in Chapter 2 when we were looking for the .profile and .cshrc files. Try it in any directory and you will see that the first two files in the list are always . (dot) and .. (dot dot). dot refers to the directory itself; dot dot has the connection back to the parent directory - the next one up the tree.

## ls -t List by Time

This lists files in date order, latest first, rather than the normal alphabetical order. This is very handy for tracking down the files that you were using in your last working session if you have forgotten their names.

### Combining Options

Options may be combined by writing the code letters in a continuous list after the dash. The order is not important - where display styles clash, the dominant one will always win however the command is written. When you want maximum information about a directory try this:

```
$ls -alF     { all, long and File types }
total 495
drwxr-xr-x  9  root  sys       224 Apr 23 11:09 ./
drwxr-xr-x  9  root  sys       224 Apr 23 11:09 ../
drwxr-xr-x  2  bin   bin      1504 Apr 13 14:37 bin/
-rw-r—r—   1  root  sys     19244 Apr 13 12:15 boot
drwxr-xr-x  4  root  sys      1424 Apr 13 13:13 dev/
drwxr-xr-x  7  root  sys      1488 Apr 23 00:08 etc/
drwxrwxrwx  3  bin   bin       384 Apr 13 13:48 lib/
drwxr-xr-x  2  root  root     1024 Apr 13 13:13 lost+found/
drwxrwxrwx  3  root  root       80 Apr 23 02:41 tmp/
-rw-r—r—   1  root  sys    204975 Apr 13 12:15 unix
drwxr-xr-x 19  bin   bin       320 Apr 23 00:08 usr/
```

Similarly, for a column-wise, time-order listing you would use:

```
$ ls -Ct
```

## Selective Lists

As well as the option codes that determine *how* files are listed, **ls** can take arguments to determine *which* files are listed.

Give it the name of a directory and **ls** will list the contents of that directory. e.g. to get a long list of the tmp directory:

**$ ls -l /tmp**

Give it the name of a file, and **ls** will list it - and no other - if that file is in the current directory. Does fred exist?

**$ ls fred**
fred: Not Found

You can check the existence of several files at a time by giving their names in a list.

**$ ls fox fax fred**
fox
fax
fred: Not found

You can also use metacharacters (the Unix equivalent of DOS' wildcards) to list a selected sub-set of files, but we'll leave that and deal with it along with other aspects of file management, in the next chapter.

## Making Directories

If you are going to use your Unix system properly, you should organise your files into a set of sub-directories, one for each category of file. How you define a category is up to you, and will depend upon what you are doing. As a student, you might have a directory for each module of your course; in a business environment, files might be organised by department, by project, by type of client, or whatever. This does not have to be done immediately. You can make or remove directories at any time, and it's simple enough to move files from one to another to reorganise them. But you do need to make a couple of directories now - partly for practice, partly because you'll need them to follow later examples.

## mkdir - Make Directory

First, go back to your home directory with a straight **cd**. To make a directory, you use the command **mkdir**, giving it the chosen name. We are going to make two, called examples and temp.

```
$ mkdir examples
$ mkdir temp
```

You will notice that, as usual, Unix doesn't bother to tell you when it has successfully performed a command. To see for yourself that the directories have been created, call up **ls**. Their names will appear along with your files.

```
$ ls
examples
fox
fax
temp              { your vi summary file should be here as well }
```

## rmdir - Remove Directory

'examples' will be used to store files created in later examples. 'temp' is very temporary. It is there to give you a chance to get rid of it. The command to remove a directory is **rmdir**. You must, of course, give it the directory name, and it will only be performed if the directory is empty.

```
$ rmdir temp$
```

Sorry. We'll shortly be needing a directory called temp after all. You know how to set it up.

# Paths, Files and Directories

To identify a directory or a file that is in your current directory - i.e. where you are at the time - all you need is its name. If you want one that is elsewhere in the system, you must also specify its **path**. This can be done in two ways - either the full path, starting at the root, or by tracking from where you are now to where the file is kept.

**Figure 4.2**

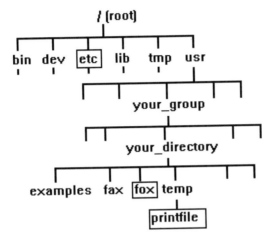

Assume that you are currently in your 'examples' sub-directory and that you are interested in the 'etc' directory and in two files - 'fox' in your main directory, and 'printfile' in your 'temp' sub-directory. Using the paths from the root, these can be identified by:

```
/etc
/usr/your_group/your_directory/fox
/usr/your_group/your_directory/temp/printfile
```

Tracking from your current position the paths become:

```
../../../../etc        {up 4 levels and down into etc}
../fox                 {up one level and there it is}
../temp/printfile      {up one level, across and down again}
```

With a nearby directory, it is simpler to track a route from where you are. With a distant one, it is simpler to work from the root.

# Chapter 5

# File Management

The huge advantage that computer files have over paper-based ones is that it is so easy to keep them organised. A moment's thought and a few seconds typing is all it takes to copy, move, rename or remove a file - or a whole set of them.

### cp - Copy a File

The **cp** command can be used in two ways - to create a second, renamed, copy of a file, or to copy a file into another directory. For operations of the first type, Unix needs two items of information - the name of the original file and the name that the copy is to be called. These items - arguments in the jargon - are written after the command, separated by spaces.

```
$ cd             { go home }
$ cp fox fox.bak
```

This creates a backup copy of your fox file, and puts it in your current directory as you haven't said otherwise.

```
$ cp fox examples/fox.bak
```

As the path is included in the name, this **cp** will create the copied file in the specified directory, and call it 'fox.bak'.

```
$ cp fox examples
```

This time the directory is specified, but there is no name for the new file. The copy will be placed in 'examples' but still called 'fox'. We are now using **cp** in its second way, and there is an important variation here. For cross-directory copying, the command has this general form:

**cp filelist  destination**

The *filelist* can be a set of named files or a wildcard expression. (See next page.) The *destination* is a simple directory name. You cannot change filenames when doing a multiple copy - not even to add a '.bak' to the end of them all.

**$ cp fox fax fix temp**
fix: Not found

When Unix performs this command, it will check that the last argument, 'temp', is a valid directory name, then work through 'fox', 'fax' and 'fix' attempting to copy each into 'temp'.

**$ cp temp/\* examples**

Here the wildcard asks for all files in the 'temp' directory to be copied into 'examples'.

Please run through these examples, if you haven't already done so. You will need the directory structure and contents shown here in later examples. (Any extra files won't matter.)

**Figure 5.1**

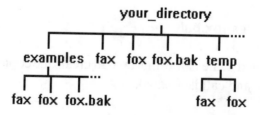

# Metacharacters, Wildcards and Filenames

If you have used DOS systems, you will have met **wildcards** - characters that can stand for any others, just as wildcards (or jokers) can in a pack of playing cards. In Unix, they are called **metacharacters** and work in the same way - only more so. As 'metacharacters' is something of a mouthful and takes a lot of typing, from here on out, I'll refer to them as 'wildcards'. There are four that you should know about:

* \* stands for any set of characters;
* ? replaces any single character;
* [] enclose a set of alternative characters.

Use these in a situation where Unix is expecting a filename - or a set of filenames - and it will take the wildcard expression and expand it into a list of names. Combine them with real characters to specify limited sets of names. e.g.

| Expression | Expands into.. |
|---|---|
| **f\*** | Any name starting with 'f' |
| **\*.txt** | Any name with '.txt' at the end |
| **.\*** | Any name starting with '.' |
| **f?x** | 'fox', 'fax', and any similar |
| **????** | Any name of four characters |
| **f[ao]x** | Either 'fax' or 'fox' |
| **jan[1-5]** | 'jan1', 'jan2', 'jan3', 'jan4', 'jan5' |

The brackets are probably the least used of the wildcards. Note that you can either bracket a fixed list of characters - **[abc]** standing for either a, b or c; or a set described by its limits - **[a-e]** stands for a, b, c, d or e.

Practice using wildcards with **ls** - you can see instantly whether you are forming the expressions correctly, and you can't do any damage!

The examples below are based on a directory containing these files and sub-directories:

```
.login    .profile    chap1.bak chap1.txt  chap2.bak chap2.txt
chp3.txt examples    fax         fax.bak    fox         fred
temp    w           wholist    x          yz
```

**$ ls -C ***       { all files except the .names }
```
chap1.bak    chap1.txt   chap2.bak chap2.txt   chp3.txt
examples
fax       fax.bak     fox    fred   temp w
wholist   x           yz
```

**$ls -C f***        { all starting with f }
```
fax       fax.bak     fox    fred
```

**$ls -C *.txt**        { all ending in .txt }
```
chap1.txt chap2.txt chap3.txt
```

**$ls -C ?**            { single character names }
```
w x
```

**$ ls -C f?x***        { any starting f something x }
```
fax       fax.bak     fox
```

**$ls -C ????**         { any four character name }
```
fred
temp:
fax       fox
```

In that last example, the expression generated the name of a sub-directory, and **ls -C temp** command lists its contents.

## rm - Remove a File

Use with care! **rm** works instantly and is strictly one-way. If you remove a file by mistake, you will only be able to get it back if your system administrator has it on the back-up tapes. As back-ups are normally done overnight, there's little prospect of recovering a file created and removed on the same day.

The command takes a single file, a list or a wildcard expression as its argument. Try these examples - note the changes of directory.

```
$ cd temp          { into your temp directory }
$rm fox
$ls
fax                { fox has gone }
$ cd ../examples   { up and across to examples }
$ rm f?x           { or rm fox fax }
$ ls
fox.bak
```

The **ls** commands are not necessary. They are simply there to show you that the files really have been removed. The only feedback you will normally get is a complaint if you ask it to remove a directory or a non-existent file.

Watch what happens when you try it - and don't miss out the line that copies everything from your main directory into examples. You are about to wipe your directory clean, and without those copies, you'll lose your hard-won files.

```
$ cd                       { back to home directory }
$ rm fred                  { or any other unused name }
fred: not found
$ cp * examples            { copy everything before ...}
cp : <examples> directory  { can't copy that }
cp : <temp> directory      { or that either }
$ rm *                     { now zap the lot! }
rm : examples directory
rm : temp directory
$ cp examples/* .          { and copy it all back again }
```

(Note the '.' at the end of the last command. When used in a path definition, the dot means 'current directory'.)

Never do **rm** * again unless you are absolutely sure that you mean it!

## mv - Move or Rename a File

Using **mv** has exactly the same effect as a **cp** followed by a **rm**. The rules for its use are therefore much the same.

If you are using it to rename files, they must be processed one at a time as the old and new names must be individually specified.

### $ mv fox quickbrown

The file 'fox' has now had its name changed to 'quickbrown' but is otherwise exactly the same.

Where **mv** is being used to relocate files, give it a list of names or a wildcard expression and end the command with the target directory.

### $ mv fax quickbrown temp

This will move both 'fax' and 'quickbrown' to your 'temp' directory. Check and see:

```
$ ls                    { in your Home directory }
fox.bak                 { you may have more here }
$cd temp
$ ls
fox  quickbrown         { and in here }
$ cd                    { back Home again }
$ mv temp/* .           { move them back home }
$ mv * temp             { and shift the lot out again}
mv : <examples> directory
mv : <temp> directory
$
```

As usual, Unix only tells you about the things it can't do. Look into 'temp' and you will find all the old Home files there.

## pg - Paged Display of Text Files

Here's an alternative to **cat** for displaying text files on screen. **pg** is the one to choose when you are looking at large files as it runs the display one page (screenful) at a time. Stick to **cat** for shorter ones as **pg** is more complex and therefore slower.

**pg** pauses at the end of each screenful and waits for your command. These include quite sophisticated facilities for searching for text items and for moving backwards and forwards within the text to selected lines. We'll leave these to Chapter 12. For most of us, for most of the time, the only commands we need to know are these:

```
[Space Bar]      - display next page
[Q] or [Del]     - quit
[H]              - display command summary
```

You will need a good-sized text file to test this. If you haven't got one to hand, create one now by redirecting the long listing of a big directory into a file. There's plenty up in the 'bin'. Send its listing to a file called 'binfile' with this line:

```
$ ls -l /bin > binfile
$ pg binfile          { now you can test pg }
```

## file - What Type is It?

The **file** command looks at a file, or set of files, and takes an educated guess as to the nature of the file(s). Try it on a single file and on the whole directory:

```
$ file fox                  { tell me about fox }
fox:          ascii text
$file *                     { tell me about all the files }
examples:     directory
fax:          ascii text
fox:          ascii text
fox.bak:      ascii text
temp:         directory
```

**file** can recognise executable programs and data files, and can distinguish between different types of text files - shell scripts and programs in other languages, English and plain ascii text. It makes the odd mistake, but is nevertheless a quicker way of checking a file's type that using **cat** or **pg** to view it on screen. It is also a lot safer. If you use either of these to display a program or data file, the command will cheerfully send all the characters to the screen, including those that are non-printable. You can fairly guarantee that at least one of these will be a control character that renders the terminal unusable. (See Chapter 8 to get out of that one.)

We'll come back to **file** in Chapter 10.

## du - Disk Usage

Though there won't be a set maximum for the amount of storage you can use, disk space is not unlimited. Find out from your supervisor how much space you could reasonably be allowed to occupy, then check your disk usage with this command.

```
% du
42    ./PASCAL/
2     ./.elm/
14    ./Mail/
2     ./temp/
14    ./learning/
34    ./language/pascal/
2     ./language/vi/
38    ./language/
2     ./home.pas/
150   ./
```

It shows the disk usage of each directory, and the overall total, with the values given in **blocks**. Each of these will be 512 bytes, or half a Kilobyte, so divide by 2 to get the total K. In this example, the user is occupying 75K of disk space. If you find that you are at - or over - your limit, then that **du** breakdown shows you where to try first when looking for savings.

Note: **du** is not a System V standard, but is generally available.

# Good Housekeeping

**Small is beautiful.**
It's easier to find a file in a directory where the **ls** list fits on one screen than in one where the list fills several screens. But how many is a screenful? With **ls -C** you can fit over a 100 on a screen; with **ls -l** you can only fit around 24. If the name alone is enough to identify a file, then the compressed listing will do. If you want more information then you will use the long listing, and will need to keep the numbers down.

**Everything in its place.**
Have separate directories for each area of your work. If you create a file in the wrong directory - move it. If a directory becomes over-full, set up a new sub-directories and move sets of files into it.

**But don't over-organise.**
You will find it easier to find files and move between directories if you have only one set, all branching off from your main directory. A complex tree structure, containing directories within directories, sub-divided to the umpteenth level, can become an impassable maze.

**Group by name.**
Make full use of suffixes. Files marked '.memo', '.text', '.bak', '.data' are easily recognised and can be copied and moved in bulk with wildcards. But take the grouping beyond that and get the same bulk file management by starting all related files in the same way. For instance, use a client's initials to prefix the memos, letters and reports.

**Keep it clean.**
Remove unwanted files as you go along, rather than letting them clutter up your directories.

**When in doubt, don't.**
If you are not certain that a file is unwanted, rather than remove it completely, move it into a temporary directory. Check this from time to time, making a note of the files' dates. Any that have not been touched in recently are presumably unwanted and can be removed.

# Chapter 6

# Working with the System

In this chapter, the emphasis is on your interaction with the system. We'll be looking at ways of getting help, redirecting inputs and outputs, pipes and some other tweaks you can apply to command lines, and take a first look at shell scripts.

## Manuals and the On-line Manual

The manuals supplied with Unix systems are generally very full and thorough. Unfortunately, they are also heavy going even for experienced users. This is probably inevitable as the Unix commands and utility programs are so complex and have so many options, that the documentation has to be compact if it's to be kept to a reasonable size. As it is, there will be anything up to a dozen hefty loose-leaf tomes on your system administrator's shelves. Two of the manuals are of interest to the ordinary user.

The **User Guide** gives an overview of the system, tutorials in the use of the editors **ed** and **vi**, and an introduction to shell programming. If you want to be aUnix programmer, you should have this on your reading list.

The **User Reference** describes the commands and utilities. This is the one to turn to if you have problems, or when you have mastered the basics and want to start exploring the possibilities of the system. If it is not easily accessible, that doesn't matter, as you can read the same information on your screen.

**man** - the on-line manual.

To read up on any command, simply type **man** and the command name. The display is normally paged, for easy reading, and the information is laid out in a standard format:

**Name** and brief definition;

**Synopsis** of usage with list of options - with **ls**, for example, it looks like this:

**ls [-abcCdfFgilLmnopqrRstux]** [filenames]

Anything in square brackets is optional. Where there is a list of option letters all bracketed together, as here, it means that any combination of them can be used with the command.

**Description** of how it works and what it does - with some commands this is very clear, with others it is either terse or technical or both;

**Options** describe the effect of each;

**Examples** show how the command is used and covers key options;

**Files** gives those that are used by the command, and any temporary files created by it;

**See Also** lists the related commands and relevant sections of the Reference Manual;

There may also be sections headed **Bugs**, if any are known; **Diagnostics**, where there are error messages; and **Warnings**, where a misused command may have particularly unwanted effects.

## Input and Output

One of the key concepts in Unix is that of standard input and output. This was touched on earlier, in "Instant Files" at the end of Chapter 2, but is so important that it is worth a closer look now.

Unix assumes, unless told otherwise, that the input comes from the keyboard and the output goes to the monitor. This is all quite reasonable and shouldn't cause any raised eyebrows. The important point is that Unix is just as happy to accept the input from a file and/or to send the output to a file. This is known as I/O (Input/Output) redirection and is managed via the symbols < and >.

**Output redirection** has been covered earlier, but to remind yourself of how it works, Try this. It will redirect the output of **ls** into a file called 'lsfile'. The space between the redirector '>' and the filename is optional, but makes the line more readable.

### $ ls -l > lsfile

The directory contents are now on file and can be printed or read on screen with **cat** or **pg**. Use redirection like this whenever you want to retain a permanent record of a program's output.

Redirection can also be used with **cat** in two different and interesting ways. In its simple version, this command will display one or more files on screen.

```
$ cat fox fax
The quick brown fox jumped over the lazy dog
My faxed joke won a pager in the cable tv quiz show
```

Redirect the output and it will join the source files together to create a new file. This is the simplest way to merge text files.

```
$cat fox fax > combined
$ ls
combined    examples fax fox fox.bak    temp
$cat combined
The quick brown fox jumped over the lazy dog
My faxed joke won a pager in the cable tv quiz show
```

If you don't give **cat** a source file, then it will take its input from the keyboard. This may not appear to be a lot of use, but combined with output redirection it can be a quick way of creating short files.

```
$ cat > test
Type in a line of text [Return]
and another one or two [Return]
then end with Ctrl-D
[Ctrl]-[D]                    {Press [Ctrl]- now}
$ cat test
Type in a line of text
and another one or two
then end with Ctrl-D
```

You can erase mistakes while you're on the same line, but there's no means of editing a line after you have pressed [Return]. Which rather raises the question of what use is such a rough and ready means of file-creation? Well, it's quick, and if what you are writing is very short or the odd error is immaterial, then it can be handy. There are two situations in particular where you might use **cat** instead of **vi** - writing memos to send in the mail (see next chapter) and writing simple shell scripts (see below).

If instead of a single redirector, you use a double **>>**, the output (from file or keyboard) is **appended** to the end of an existing file. Try it:

```
$ cat >>test
Here is a bit more text
[Ctrl] [D]                    { end the keyboard input }
$ cat test
Type in a line of text
and another one or two
then end with Ctrl-D
Here is a bit more text
$
```

To demonstrate **Input redirection**, we really need a program or command that takes keyboard input, and everything we've covered so far either takes no input at all or works on files. There's one exception that we could use - the **passwd** command. When you run this, your conversation with the computer will go something like this:

```
$ passwd
Old password: fred123          {your entries are invisible}
Enter new password: letmein
Re-enter new password: letmein
```

There are some variations of this, so run it first to find out exactly how yours works. Make a note of the keystrokes that you make - including [Return] presses. Now write these into a file, using **cat**:

```
$ cat > passfile
fred123[Return]    {or whatever your current password is}
letmein[Return]    {or whatever new password you want}
letmein[Return]    { [Ctrl]-[D] to finish }
$
```

We can now use Input redirection to pass this keystroke sequence to the **passwd** program.

```
$ passwd < passfile
```

If you are a programmer, try using Input redirection as an alternative to keyboard entry on your own programs. As it is no longer interactive - i.e. you don't respond directly to the prompts - it can be tricky getting everything in the right order, but if you can overcome that hurdle, this can be a convenient way of getting test data into a program during development.

## Pipelines

One of the features of Unix that gives it such power, is the ease with which commands and utility programs can be linked together. The output of one program can be the input for another - directly, without having to go through an intermediate file. In the jargon, you are setting up a **pipeline**, or more briefly **pipe**, and the symbol that links the commands is the vertical bar '|'. (This is usually located on the backslash key.)

Suppose that you wanted to examine the full listing of the '/bin' directory.

This is far too long to fit on one screen. You could redirect the output from **ls -l** to a file, then display that file with **pg**. Alternatively, you could pipe it with:

```
$ ls -l /bin | pg
```

Pipes are a key part of Unix's building-block approach. Instead of having a few highly complex programs to handle file management and text-processing, it has a very large set of single-purpose utilities. These are often referred to as **filters,** where they take a stream of data, perform some process on it and pass on the result - either to the screen, a file, or another filter. By linking them together through pipes, you can perform an almost infinite variety of sophisticated processing tasks. Paged directory listing is a simple, though useful, example of what can be done.

A development from the simple pipe is the **tee** - the T-junction in the plumbing analogy. This splits the output from a command, sending it to the screen, as normal, with a copy going either to a file or to the next command in the pipeline. It can not be used as a stand-alone command, but only as a pipe fitting.

```
$ ls -l | tee lsfile
```

This will give you a screen display of the directory list, and create a file called 'lsfile'.

It is a valuable facility for programmers, as it allows them to collect a copy of their screen displays in a file, while viewing them on screen. Note that it does only copy the *output* from the program. Anything typed in during execution is not picked up by the **tee** file.

There are two options. **-i** makes it ignore interrupts, and is rarely necessary; **-a** appends the output to an existing file, rather than overwriting it. For example, we could redirect today's date to a file, then append the current directory listing to it:

```
$ date > today
$ ls -l | tee -a today
```

It may be worth noting that the bar | is not the only possible connector in a pipeline. The carat ^ is a straightforward alternative - the effects are identical. If you join commands with **&&**, the following command will only be executed if the preceding one is successful; similarly, with ‖ the later command is only run if the earlier one fails. (See Chapter 9 for more on these and look out for other examples of pipelines further on in the book.)

## Running Commands in the Background

Some jobs can take a while. Compiling text files into programs, or running programs that perform complex calculations or sort large sets of values or update lengthy datafiles can all lock up your terminal for a noticeable amount of time. This can be a good excuse for a coffee break, but you may want to get on with other jobs. If this is the case, you can push the slow program into the background, where it will tick over by itself, and leave you free to run other commands. All you need to do is tack an ampersand (**&**) on the end of the command line.

```
$ cob update.cbl -o update &  { compiling one Cobol program }
$ vi printout.cbl             { and off to edit the next }
```

## Lists of Commands

If you want to run through a set of commands, one immediately after the next, you can write into a single command line. Use a semi-colon to separate each command from the next. It won't save you any time or typing, but at least you won't have to wait for each to finish before giving the next command.

```
$ date ; pwd ; ls -lt
Fri 14th Nov 15:34
/usr/staff/mac/Cobol
.....
```

If you want to run any of the listed commands in the background, just include the ampersand before the semi-colon.

```
$ update & ; lp printfile ; who
```

In this list, only the 'update' program will be sent to the background:

If you want to run *all* of the list in the background, then enclose the whole set in brackets and add the ampersand to the end. This list will compile a C program, sending its error report to a file, then print the file:

```
$ (cc quicksort.c > errfile ; lp errfile ) &
```

## Shell Scripts

Shell scripts are programs written in the shell's own language. They can be as complex as programs written in any other language, but a script does not have to be complex to be useful. A simple script may consist of a straightforward list of commands, and when it is executed, each command will be performed in turn. This is the sort we are interested in.

In this first example you will create a short file, consisting of one command, then pass it to **sh** the (Bourne) shell program. This reads the script and executes any commands it finds.

```
$ cat > list    { make a file called list }
ls -l           { containing this command }
[Ctrl]-[D]      { end the cat input }

$ sh list       { pass list to the shell }
drwxr-xr— 2 mac    staff      128  Apr 11 19:34 examples
-rw-r—r— 2 mac     staff       44  Apr 11 19:57 fax
-rw-r—r— 2 mac     staff       44  Apr 19 13:52 fax.bak
-rw-r—r— 2 mac     staff       44  Apr 11 16:34 fox
-rw-r—r— 2 mac     staff       44  Apr 11 17:46 fox.bak
-rw-r—r— 2 mac     staff        6  Apr 20 18:53 list
drwxr-xr— 2 mac    staff      128  Apr 11 19:47 temp
```

This may seem a little pointless, as it takes longer to set up the script than it does to type the direct command. However, scripts makes good sense where you are regularly using a set of commands, or where a command line that contains lengthy filenames.

The following script will find the date, checks the current path, then list files in date order. It needs three commands **date, pwd** and **ls -lt**. We'll use the initials to name the script 'dpl'.

```
$ cat >dpl
date
pwd
ls -lt
[Ctrl]-[D]
```

'**sh dpl**' will now find the date, current path and directory listing.

## Executable Scripts

We can dispense with the **sh** command and run the script directly if we make it executable. And that is a lot easier than it sounds. All we need to do to make this executable is to change its permissions. Look closely at the file's listing as it is at the moment. If you create a text file, whether with **cat, vi,** or any other editor, it will normally have the permissions set so that you have read/write access and others have read-only access. Use the 'long list' version of **ls** to see the permissions:

```
$ ls -l dpl
-rw-r—r— 2 mac    staff    15 Apr 20 21:16 dpl
```

## chmod - Change Permission Mode

The 'group' and 'others' permissions may be different on yours, but the first set will be the same. That **rw-** states that you can read and write the file, but not execute it. To change it to **rwx** we use the **chmod** command. This needs to know the changes that are to be made, and the files that are affected.

The changes definition is in three parts:

**who:**        **u** (user/owner) **g** (group members) **o** (others) **a** (all)
**which way**: **+** (add) **-** (remove) **=** (set)
**what mode**: **r** (read) **w** (write) **x** (execute)

These can be combined freely within the who/which/what format, with settings for different classes of user separated by commas:

| Change | Effect |
|--------|--------|
| **u+x** | add execute permission for owner |
| **go-rw** | remove read & write for group & others |
| **a+x** | add execute permission for user, group & others |
| **u=rwx,g=x** | full access for you, execute for your group |

Give yourself execute permission for the script, check that the changes have been made:

```
$chmod u+x dpl
$ ls -l dpl
-rwxr—r— 2 mac    staff    15 Apr 20 21:16 dpl
```

You can now execute it by simply typing the name:

```
$ pdl
Fri Apr 24 12:45:36 GMT 1992
/usr/staff/mac
-rwxr—r— 2 mac   staff     15   Apr 20 21:16 dpl
drwxr-xr— 2 mac  staff    128   Apr 11 19:34 examples
-rw-r—r— 2 mac   staff     44   Apr 11 19:57 fax
-rw-r—r— 2 mac   staff     44   Apr 19 13:52 fax.bak
-rw-r—r— 2 mac   staff     44   Apr 11 16:34 fox
-rw-r—r— 2 mac   staff     44   Apr 11 17:46 fox.bak
-rw-r—r— 2 mac   staff      6   Apr 20 18:53 list
drwxr-xr— 2 mac  staff    128   Apr 11 19:47 temp
```

We'll return to shell scripts in Chapter 16.

# Chapter 7

# Working with Others

Now that Unix is available for PCs, some people will be working alone on their own individual machines, but the vast majority of us are working alongside others on multi-user systems. Sharing resources with others has its limitations, but it also creates opportunities. As well as sharing resources you can also share ideas and files. In this chapter we will concentrate on the opportunities, with just a few brief words about the limitations at the end.

## Sharing Ideas

### Electronic Mail

Electronic mail is fashioned along the lines of the traditional postal service, but with some added advantages. As with the normal post, e-mail is not delivered to people's hand but to their mailbox, which means that it does not matter if they are in or not at the time. You can look in your mailbox at any point, read messages or not, as you fancy, then put them back into the box or into safe storage elsewhere, or throw them away.

The key advantages claimed for e-mail are that messages are sent almost instantly - there's no waiting for the postman; copies of a message can be sent to as many people as you like, without retyping; and it's free, as there are no postmen's wages to pay. e-mail is also definitely easier to ignore than letters and memos. Whether this is an advantage or a disadvantage depends upon the quality of the correspondence over your system. When people know about e-mail and realise how easy it is to use it, there is normally a significant increase in the quantity of correspondence within the organisation. Some of this will be valuable, much trivial.

There may well be several e-mail programs available on your system, some more sophisticated than others. The simplest, and the one which is certain to be present on any system, is **mail**. You may also find **mailx** or **elm**, or have one as part of a larger office automation package. Though they will differ in their commands and their range of features, all e-mail programs share the same basic features.

When a message is first sent to a user, it will be stored in a temporary mailbox. This is a file, normally located in the '/usr/mail' directory. Any new messages will be added to this file as they arrive, and they will all be kept safe until you choose to deal with them. When you login, on most systems, Unix will check the mail directory and if it finds a file with your name, it will inform you that you have mail. You can access the file at any point during a work session by calling up one or other of the e-mail programs.

## mail - No Frills E-Mail

This program takes the cheap and cheerful approach. It has a simple, limited command set, but is very handy for a quick scan of the mail or for dropping someone a short memo. To check your mailbox, type **mail**. If it is empty, you'll be told 'No mail', otherwise the first (oldest) message will be displayed.

> **$ mail**
> From jill Fri Apr 24 12:38 GMT 1992
> Don't forget the team meeting on Monday 27th at 11.30.
> Next year's budget top of the agenda.
> Jill
>
> **?**

The **?** at the bottom of the screen tells you that mail is waiting for a command. There are only 10, and all accessed by typing a single character and [Return]. The save, delete and forward commands all work on the current message. There are two methods of saving messages. The 's' command saves the whole message, complete with its header line; 'w' chops off the header and saves only the text. In either case, the message will be added to the file 'mbox' in your home directory, unless you specifically tell it otherwise. (This file can then be edited with **vi** or any other editor.) All messages remain in your system mailbox, and will still be there next time you run **mail**, until they are deleted.

| Command | Effect |
|---|---|
| **[Return] or +** | Display next message |
| **p** | Redisplay last message |
| **-** | Display previous message |
| **d** | Delete |
| **s** | Save in the standard mbox file |
| **s** *filename* | Save in the named file |
| **w [***filename***]** | As save, but without the message header |
| **m [***user***]** | Forward a copy on to the named user |
| **q** | Quit |
| **x** | Exit - but cancel any deletes |
| ***** | Display command summary |

Messages for mailing can be prepared beforehand or typed "on-line", while mail is running. The on-line method is fine for short messages. Call up mail and give the name(s) of the users who are to get copies. Type your message, pressing [Return] at the end of each line. When you have finished, press [Ctrl]-[D].

**$ mail jill bill sue**        { copies to three users }
**Do you know an easy way to get random numbers [Return]**
**I need 1000 to test my statistics program [Return]**
**[Ctrl]-[D]**

As there's no means of editing a line once you have pressed [Return] on it, this approach is not suitable for longer messages. Instead, write your message with **vi** or any other text editor, then pass it to mail using I/O redirection. Here, mail takes its input from a text file called 'memo'.

**$ mail jill bill sue < memo**

## **write** - Two-Way Communication

Though mail is transmitted instantly across the system, there's no guarantee that the recipient will read it instantly - rather the reverse. People tend to check their mailboxes at the start of a session then ignore them for the rest of the day. If you want immediate feedback, or a two-way conversation, then you need a different approach. The surest method is to get out of your seat and go and talk to them directly, or give them a ring - but we can also manage it through the Unix system, if conditions are right.

The **write** command copies text directly to the terminal of another user. It first sends a header note to the recipient, to let them know who is trying to establish communication; e.g. "Message from dick on tty15". If the recipient agrees, a two-way link is created. After that, everything typed by the writer is echoed on the other's screen, until the writer ends the link with a [Ctrl]-[D]. That's a bare outline of what write does. Putting it to practical use is a little more involved.

**write** must be used co-operatively, if it is to work successfully. First, the other user must be open to incoming messages. The command **mesg y** sets you open to receive, while **mesg n** blocks writing. **write** can be intrusive. Not everyone appreciates having a message pop up on the screen while they are trying to edit a text file. It won't actually corrupt the file, but it can break the concentration.

Secondly, the other user must write back to you to establish the two-way link. Though the communication is two-way, there is only one screen at either end and your typing and your correspondent's will become garbled if you both write at the same time. This brings us to the last point - you must agree to take turns. The normal convention is to write 'o' (over) at the end of a message and 'oo' (over and out) when you finish.

A typical write session might follow the pattern shown below. Notice that the sender, Mark, waits for Jill to acknowledge his approach by writing to him, before he sends the first message.

| Mark's terminal | Jill's terminal |
|---|---|
| **$write jill** | Message from mark on tty15 |
| Message from jill on tty42 | **$write mark** |
| **Is Dick over there with you?** | Is Dick over there with you? |
| o | o |
| No. Can John help instead? | **No. Can John help instead?** |
| o | o |
| **Yes. Ask him to come please** | Yes. Ask him to come please |
| **oo** | oo |

# Sharing Files

There are essentially two approaches to sharing files. You can either send copies of a file to other users, or arrange for others to have access to a single file. Unix being as flexible as it is, there are several ways of implementing both approaches. At this point, we'll stick to the simplest.

## Sending Copies

If you want to send someone a copy of a *text* file, the simplest solution is probably to use the mail. I/O redirection will let us take the mail "message" from the file. Suppose you had a sales report, called 'salerep', to send to Freda. You could do this:

### $ mail freda < salesrep

When it gets to the other end, Freda can read it directly on the mail, or save it to a named file and perhaps print it later. The mail system will have stuck a header line on the file, but that can be removed easily enough if it is a nuisance.

If the file contains *non-text data*, or is a *compiled program*, then the mail method is not really feasible. The header line will still be there and the file will be difficult, or impossible, to edit. The answer here is to look for a directory that is open to both you and your colleagues. You can then copy the file into it, they can copy it out and they will have full ownership of their copy. It may be that there is a common directory open to all of your group.

If not, the '/tmp' directory, at the top of the system, is always open to all.

Send a copy to '/tmp' with a line like this:

$ **cp salesrep /tmp**

Then other users can get a copy by:

$ **cp /tmp/salesrep .**

This line will copy the file into the user's current directory, identified by the dot, and will retain its original name. If its destination is elsewhere, then replace the dot with the path. And if the copy is to have a different name, that also should be specified:

$ **cp /tmp/salesrep accounts/sales.fred**

Here the copy goes into the 'accounts' sub-directory, and has been renamed to remind the new owner that it came from Fred.

Sometimes a little preparatory work is needed before you copy. Usually the permissions are set by default to allow others to read - and therefore copy - a file. (Though as long as it is in your directory others cannot read it because they don't have read access to the directory.) Check the permissions on the file with **ls -l** and if necessary, use **chmod** to change them to give others read access:

$ **chmod a+r salesrep**

## In Shared Access

This is the approach to take when it is important that there is only one active copy of the file in the system. This would be the case where the file held key reference data. A business will (normally) only keep one set of account books, and several people will need access to this. If there were multiple copies of the accounts files, the transactions recorded by one person would not appear in the copies held by others.

You might also use a shared file if you were writing a report and wanted to collect people's comments on it before producing the finished copy. Their notes could be added directly to the draft file, then incorporated during a final edit.

A shared file can be in an open, common, directory or in a user's individual directory. In either case, only one person will actually own it - the user who first created it. Other users will have access to it via a *link*. Each will have an entry in their own directory, as if the file were there. It will show up with an **ls** and can be copied and moved - even removed - as if it were a real file. But it's not. It's only a link to the real file. When you remove a link, you merely close down your access to the file.

To set up the shared file, its owner must first set the permissions so that others can read and write to it. Suppose Jill has produced the first draft of the team's report. She opens up the access with:

**$chmod a+rw teamreport**   { 'teamreport' is the file }

The others can then make the link with the **ln** command. They need to give this the full path to the original file and a name by which the link will be known. It can have the same name as the original, or not, as you choose. One user might link with this:

**$ ln -s /usr/sales/jill/teamreport teamreport**

Another with this, changing the name in the process:

**$ ln -s /usr/sales/jill/teamreport jills_report**

Note that the command is usually given with the -s option, specifying that this is a symbolic link. (See below.)

To try out this technique, you'll obviously need the cooperation of someone else on the system. But have a go. You'll no doubt find a use for it before long, and it's worth learning how to do it.

**Possible Problems**

1) You may find that on your system only the administrator, or someone else with superuser access, can give the **ln** command. If this is the case, you will also need their cooperation, but it is still worth investigating.

2) The simple **ln** will only create a link between files if they are part of the same overall file structure, within one device. (Where the 'device' is typically a partition on a hard disk.) As all the users' directories are generally on the same device, this shouldn't cause a problem. The alternative **ln -s** sets up a *symbolic link* between files, and this overcomes the barriers between devices. So, if **ln** doesn't work, try **ln -s**.

# Chapter 8

# Help!

As a new Unix user, you will no doubt make mistakes and sometimes find yourself in situations that you do not fully understand. (Actually, that applies to almost all Unix users, new and old.) That's how it should be, for if you don't make mistakes it can only be that you are not trying anything new and therefore not learning. Fortunately, there are some simple techniques that will solve most problems.

First, try to identify your problem. Is it one of the "How do I get out of this?" type, or is it a more fundamental "What's happening?"

## How do I get out of this?

You are stuck in a program which you didn't mean to get into, or have forgotten how to get out of. It is all too easy to set a program running by accident. If, for instance, you type **dc** in place of **cd**, then instead of changing directory, you will start the "desk calculator". (Don't let the friendly title fool you. This beast is only for mathematicians who can handle reverse Polish notation. See Chapter 15.)

Different programs have different exit routes, but one or other of these keystrokes will work most of the time:

| | |
|---|---|
| **[Ctrl]-[D]** | the normal end of session signal |
| **[Del]** | interrupts many programs |
| **[Q]** or **[X]** | common Quit or eXit keys |
| **[Esc] [Z][Z]** | the exit from vi |

If none of these work, you might be tempted to turn off the terminal. Don't bother - it won't have any effect. The program will still be running when you turn it back on. No, if all else fails, you'll have to **kill** it.

## Processes and how to Kill them

When a program is running on the system, it is known as a **process**. The command **ps** will tell you what processes you are running anywhere on the system - i.e. at any terminal. This is important, because if your terminal is locked up in a program, you can't run **ps** from there. Go to a second terminal and login. Run **ps** and see what you get. It should be run with the options **-ef** to give a full list of processes, from every terminal which you are using. The simple **ps** will only tell you about the current terminal.

```
$ ps -ef
PID      TTY  TIME  CMD
1234     tty15 00:02sh
1267     tty15 00:01        lockup      { or whatever }
1320     tty17 00:01sh
1321     tty17 00:01ps
```

The display shows the process identification numbers (PID), the terminal on which they are running (TTY), the cumulative time that the system has spent on them (TIME) and the program or command name (CMD). You should find that you have two **sh** or **csh** shell programs - one for each terminal, the **ps** command, and the cause of your problems. Here, the user is on terminals 15 and 17, and it is **lockup** on that is causing the trouble.

If a process appears on your **ps** list, you own it and you can **kill** it. This command takes no options, but does want a signal number. Without getting technical about it, all this means is that you have to give the number **-9** to guarantee a hit. **kill** also needs to know the PID of the process.

```
$ kill -9 1267     { kills "lockup" on terminal 15}
$ ps               { check that it has gone }
PID      TTY  TIME  CMD
1234     tty15 00:02sh
1320     tty17  00:01  sh
1321     tty17  00:01  ps
```

If your **ps** check shows that the locking program is still running, it may just be that it took a little while to die. Wait a moment and try again. If it is still there, you must have mistyped the PID. **kill** it again.

Check back to you original terminal and you should find that you are back to your normal prompt.

# What's Happening?

There is, of course, more than one answer to this question, and the sheer scope of Unix and the variations between installations make it impossible for any book to provide all the answers. However, there are certain common patterns and you should be able to recognise them and to know whether you can handle them yourself or need to call for help.

## A Suitable Case

### Symptom
You've just logged in and when you type in LOWER CASE it comes out in capitals, and when you type in \C\A\P\I\T\A\L\S there's a backslash in front of the letters.

### Probable Cause
You had the [Caps Lock] on when you logged in. The system saw your capitals, when it had expected lower case, and decided that your terminal was one of the old ones that only uses capital letters.

### Possible Cure
Logout. Makes sure the [Caps Lock] is off, and login again.

## Dead Screens Tell no Tales

### Symptom
The screen is totally blank and does not respond to anything you type.

### Probable Cause
Something's been knocked loose or turned off. Some monitors have

exposed switches that can be clipped by a stray book, and cables can sometimes be snagged by people as they squeeze past - or by your own feet under the desk!

## Possible Cure

Check the obvious first. Is the monitor still turned on? Next look at the cable connections - but don't fiddle with them! There should be three cables plugged into the back of the terminal - all easy to identify. One will be from the keyboard; a second from the mains supply; the third carries the connection to the central computer. Do they look secure? If possible, trace the mains lead back to its socket and check that the power is turned on. If everything appears to be as it should, and there's still no joy, call for a technician.

## Terminal Disaster

### Symptom

The screen is alive, but not well. There are garbled characters on it, and when you type, it is either ignored or garbled.

### Probable Cause

You have used **cat** or **vi** to display a program or data file on screen. Unlike plain text files, these are likely to contain characters outside the usual printing range.

Terminals are designed to respond to certain control characters. Character 10, for example, moves the cursor down to the next line; character 8 moves the cursor left and may (or not, depending upon the terminal) rub out the previous letter. Other control characters will clear the screen, turn special effects on and off, and there's always at least one that will stop the terminal from responding to your typing. These are part of the ASCII set, but are not printable, i.e. they won't be seen on the screen though their effect may well be visible.

### Possible Cure

Turn off the terminal. Wait a few seconds while the capacitors discharge and all electrical activity ceases, then turn it back on again. The screen should be clear, and if you press [Return] a couple of times, your prompt will reappear.

## Which Program?

### Symptom
You have written and (successfully) compiled a program, but when you run it, the result is completely different from what you could reasonably expect.

### Probable Cause
It could be simply that your program is wrong, but there's another possibility. If you call a program by the same name as an existing system utility, when you try to run it, you may well get the system program instead. The problem lies in your **PATH**, which tells Unix what directories it should search and in which order. It will typically look in the '/bin' and '/usr/bin' directories before it tries your current directory, and ignore your program in favour of the one it finds up there.

The **which** command will tell you which version of a program it is running, by giving you the full directory path. If you were having problems with a program called 'test', you could try:

```
$ which test
/usr/bin/test
```

This is clearly not yours!

(NB. which is not a standard System V program, but it is often included in the package.)

### Possible Cure
Use **mv** to change the name of the program and try again. To prevent the problem occuring again, you could change your PATH, so that the system tries your directories before the main '\bin's. We'll return to PATHs and how to set them in Chapter 9.

## No Response to Commands

### Symptom
You cannot see the usual shell prompt ($ or whatever), but your typing appears on screen as normal. Commands do not, however, produce the desired effect.

### Probable Cause
You are almost certainly stuck in a program.

### Possible Cure
See "How do I get out of this?"

## Crash!

### Symptom
Your terminal has locked, and glancing round you see that everybody else is in the same state.

### Probable Cause
This is a system crash. They happen occasionally, even in the best regulated organisations.

### Possible Cure
Out of your hands. Go and have a cuppa while the system administrator struggles with it.

# Part 2

# Extending Your Range

# The Shells

Whether it is the Bourne, Korn or C, the Unix shell controls your working environment, and acts as both a command line interpreter and a programming language. It will interpret your instructions one at a time as they are given at the prompt, or will work through a structured sequence of instructions that are written into a script. It's similar to Basic in this respect - though the similarities don't extend much beyond that. You've already seen that it checks command lines, calling up programs and expanding wildcards into sets of names. In the following sections we will be looking at those other features that give the shell a programming capability - its use of variables, and its limited but adequate set of words that allow it to repeat operations, test values and act conditionally on the basis of those tests. It is important to acquire at least a rudimentary understanding of shell programming at this stage if you are to make much use of the more advanced Unix operations.

The Bourne shell is present as standard in all Unix System V installations. The C shell is also found in most, and the Korn shell in an increasing number. Which one is used as your normal start-up shell depends upon your system administrator, but there is nothing to stop you invoking any other that may be present. To create a new shell use:

**sh**     for a Bourne shell;
**csh**    for a C shell;
**ksh**    for a Korn shell.

You can have any number of shells, of the same or different types, running simultaneously. Each new one will exist inside, but independently of, the previous one.

91

In practice, you are generally better off within the more user-friendly C shell for routine file management and for running applications. When you want to write shell scripts, then the Bourne shell will give you a more comprehensive language and more portable scripts. As the C shell can run Bourne scripts, there's no problem about switching between the two. If you have the Korn shell, then you have the best of both, and can stick to that.

We will start with the Bourne shell, as that is the basic standard and much of what is said about that will apply to the others, then move on to look at the special features of the C shell environment. In Chapter 16, we return to Bourne to explore shell scripts.

**Special Characters**

Take care typing these characters in a command line or script - they have special meanings for the shell:

**\* ? [ ] | ; : { } ( ) < > << >> $ = ' "**

Sometimes you will want to use the characters for themselves, or pass them through the shell and on to a command without being interpreted. In that case, the character must be 'escaped' by preceding it with a backslash. (\). For example, try this:

**$ echo \***

(The echo command displays whatever follows it - literal text or the values of variables.)

You should find that it lists the files in your current directly. The '**\***' wildcard has been expanded to become all the visible filenames. Now try:

**$ echo \\***

This time it will simply print the asterisk. The backslash has removed its special meaning.

# Chapter 9

# The Bourne Shell

If you are not already in a Bourne shell, invoke one now by typing **sh**. This sets up a new one, inside your original shell. There are a number of implications to this, but the most obvious is that when you have finished, you will first have to type **exit** to get back out of your C shell, before you can logout.

If you do login to a Bourne shell, have a look now at the '.profile' file. You should see something along the lines of this:

```
PATH=/bin:/usr/bin:/etc/:$HOME
USER=dick
MAIL=/usr/spool/mail/$USER
export PATH USER MAIL
umask 033
mesg n
```

There may be other things in there as well. In the process of defining your working environment, '.profile' sets variables - principally PATH, USER & MAIL - and runs commands. In the example, these are **umask** and **mesg**. We will take a quick look at what these two do before moving on to variables.

## umask - File Permissions

**umask** sets the default permissions for any files that you create, albeit in a roundabout way. (At least it looks roundabout from the outside, but no doubt makes programming simpler at system level.) It works by *masking*

- filtering out what is not wanted - rather than by defining what it wanted. To understand it properly, we need to go back to **chmod**. Last time we looked at this, in Chapter 6, we changed permissions by commands like:

> ## $ chmod g+wx common.prog

If you had to set all the permissions for a file, the argument string could become somewhat ungainly:

> ## $ chmod u+rwx,g=rx,o-rwx newfile
> ## $ ls -l newfile
> -rwxr-x— 1 fiona    staff        2407 Nov 10 09:48 newfile

Permissions can be set more compactly by using octal numbers to represent the codes. 'r' is worth 4, 'w' 2 and 'x' 1. Add them together to get the permissions for each category of user. Thus, the octal equivalent of that last command would be:

> ## $ chmod 750 newfile

Similarly, 744 would give you full access, but restrict your group and others to read only. Now we can go back to **umask**.

**umask** sets the number to be taken from 777 (working in octal) to define the permissions.

| base | 777 | | |
|------|-----|--------|---------|
| umask | 033 | | |
| result | 744 | giving | rwxr—r— |

## mesg - Screen Access

You should recall this from Chapter 7. It controls whether or not your terminal is open for other people to **write** to. As an unwanted message can be disruptive, it is a sensible precaution to include **mesg n** in the '.profile'. If and when you want to communicate with others via your terminal, you can open the lines with:

> ## $ mesg y

## Variables and Parameters

Like any other programming language, the shell supports the use of **variables** - named places in memory in which data can be stored. Unlike other languages, in the shell, all variables are of the same sort - simple strings of text. Numbers can be stored in them, but only as text. If you want to calculate with variables, special techniques are needed.

To assign a value to a variable, use an expression of the type:

variable=value

e.g.

**$ name=Fred**

Do not put spaces around the '='. If you do, the shell will try to treat 'name' as a command and give you a 'Not Found' message. If the value consists of more than a single word, it must be enclosed in quotes:

**$ name='Dick Turpin'**

When you want to get the value back out of the variable, its name must be preceded by a dollar sign.

```
$echo $name
Dick Turpin
$
```

Try it, and see what you get if you omit the dollar sign when echoing the value back.

To see how the shell handles numbers, set up two variables, giving them number values, and try to add them. Your screen display should be:

```
$ num1=42
$ num2=99
$ echo $num1 + $num2
42 + 99
```

As you can see, the shell does not recognise numbers as values, but as strings of text digits. It is possible to force it to evaluate a variable, and we will come back to that in Chapter 16 where we look more closely at shell programming. Often, however, there's not much point. If you wanted a calculating program, there are better languages than the shell. It is designed for manipulating commands and text files.

## The Scope of Variables

A variable normally exists only in the shell in which it was created. If you want to make its values accessible to other shells, you must force this with the **export** command. Test it with this sequence:

```
$ first=Fred              { set up two new variables }
$ surname=Jones
$ export surname          { export one of them }
$ sh                      { invoke a new shell }
$ echo $first $surname    { find out what they hold }
Jones                     { first holds nothing }
$ exit                    { leave the inner shell }
$ echo $first $surname    { check the values again }
FredJones
```

This might all seem a little hypothetical - after all, why enter a new shell if you are going to lose your variables - but it is important. It matters because when you run a shell script with **sh**, it creates a new shell to run the script. So, if you want to access variables, created at the prompt or in a script, when you are in another script, they must be exported.

## The Environment Variables

These are the ones that are built-in to the shell, and in the jargon are properly called **shell parameters**. They are maintained by the system to store information about your working environment. Some are more important than others. Some of these will have already been set for you. Some cannot, or should not, be changed. Others are a matter of personal choice and can be reset to adjust the your working environment. It is worth looking carefully at these, for the standard settings may not quite suit the way that you work.

The variables can be reset at the prompt - in which case the new setting will take effect immediately and remain active until you log out or change it again. Test your new values in this way, and when you are happy with the effects, fix them for the future by editing their settings in '.profile'. They will then be in place when you next login.

Note that the shell parameters are always written in CAPITALS, and are accessible to any inner shells that may be created.

## HOME

This stores the path to your home directory. Echo it to the screen to find your path:

   **$ echo $HOME**   {don't forget the $}

It will be something like '/usr/staff/john'

This parameter should not be changed.

## PATH

When you type in the name of a program, or give a command (and a command is simply a program provided by the system) how does Unix know where to find the program? It could be in any of your directories, up in the main 'bin' or anywhere else to which you have access.

There's a second, related problem. A typical Unix system will have hundreds of commands and utilities available to its users. If you are writing your own programs, there's a fair chance that at some time or another you will write one with the same name as a built-in one. How will Unix know whether you want your 'sort' program or the 'sort' that it's got tucked away in the bin?

The path tells the system where to look for programs, and - just as importantly - where to look first. It consists of a sequence of directory names, written in search order, and should include all the open-access system directories plus those of yours that contain programs that you might want to use. A standard path will almost certainly have been defined for you, somewhere or other. To find the current setting of the PATH variable, type this:

$ **echo $PATH**

If the standard setting is not the most suitable for the way you want to work, redefine it.

**Path definition**

A typical path definition will read:

$ **PATH=/bin:/bin/usr:.**

This follows the same pattern as any other variable definition, but look carefully at that directory name list. The names are separated by colons, with no spaces in between them.

Given this path, when you type a command, the system will look first in '/bin', then in '/usr/bin' and finally in your current directory. It stops looking, of course, as soon as it finds a program with a matching name.

The order and choice of directories to include in your path depends upon the location of program files and the type of user that you are. As the search for a match proceeds in path order, you will get a faster response from those at the start of the path. So, find out the location of the programs that you use most frequently and place their directories at the start. For most people, this will mean that the path should begins with '/bin:/usr/bin ..' which is where you will find **ls**, **rm** and similar file management commands. This is how the default paths begin on most systems.

For **business users**, who are mainly running word-processing, accounts packages or other application software, the path should start with those applications' directories.

**Programmers** will probably want their current directory - identified by the single dot (.) - early in the path. Those who intend to write their own utility programs, should store these in your main directory or a special sub-directory and write its name early in the path. The variable **$HOME** stores the route to your directory - use that in your path instead of typing the full route. e.g.

$ **PATH=.:$HOME:$HOME/utils:/bin:/usr/bin**

This puts your current directory, your main directory and your sub-directory 'utils' at the head of the search path.

The **PATH** is normally set in '.profile'.

## PS1 and PS2

Like a personalised prompt, rather than that boring '$' that everybody has? Then make your own. These parameters define the prompts. **PS1** is the normal prompt ($), **PS2** the one that you will see sometimes when you give an incomplete command line (>).

You could give yourself more interesting prompts with something along the lines of:

$ **PS1='Next job:'**
$ **PS2='And the rest of it ..'**

There's no real limit to the length of the prompt string, except the practical one. I've known students to have prompts that read 'What is your command, Oh great master of the Unixverse:' - or words to that effect.

It may massage your ego, but it doesn't leave much space across the screen for the commands!

The default prompt parameters are set by the shell, but your system manager may have set up alternatives in your '.profile'.

## MAIL

If this is set, the shell will check your mailbox when you login and inform you if there is anything in it.

The definition identifies the file in which the system stores your incoming mail. This will be labelled with your user name and will be held in the mail directory. It should look something like this:

**MAIL=/usr/spool/mail/fred**

You should find a line of this type in your '.profile' (if you have one), though on some systems it can be set at a deeper level. Echo MAIL to the screen to view your setting.

## ? - Exit Status

When a command or program has ended, it returns a value to the shell, where it is held in the parameter **?**. This value will be either 0, to signify True, or 1, signifying False, depending upon what happened within the command. Though interesting, this is irrelevant unless you specifically want to know the outcome of a command, or want an action to be conditional upon that outcome.

## cmp - File Comparison

Perhaps the clearest example of exit status comes from the **cmp** command. This compares two files, byte by byte, and either reports any differences or returns a single exit status value to tell you whether or not they are the same. Its basic shape is:

**cmp [-ls]** *file1 file2*

We will use it with the **-s** option as this suppresses the display of differing lines. We are not interested in the details, merely whether or not two files are the same.

Try it with files that you know are the same - and then again with two that are different - and test the exit status after each comparison.

```
$ cp fox fox.copy
$ cmp -s fox fox.copy
$ echo $?
0                        { They were the same }
$ cmp -s fax fax.bak     { Is the backup copy current? }
$ echo $?                { Don't forget the $ }
$ 1                      { No - they are different }
```

Having established that the backup copy is not up to date, you might now create a new backup. But the 'compare-and-copy-if-necessary' routine doesn't need you to check the exit status.

## Conditional Command Lines

A command line may contain two distinct commands, with the execution of the second being conditional upon the result of the first. There are two possible conditional links:

```
&&   Do if true (exit status = 0)
||   Do if false (exit status = 1)
```

A line which created a new backup if the old one was no longer valid would look like this:

```
$ cmp -s fox fox.bak || cp fox fox.bak
```

Similarly, a line to remove an unwanted copy would take this form:

```
$ cmp -s fox hound && rm hound
```

Lines like this can be very powerful when used in shell scripts, where you can run a whole directory through the process with the aid of variables.

# Chapter 10

# The C Shell

The C shell was developed at the University of California at Berkeley as a more user-friendly alternative to the Bourne shell. Its basic function of command line interpretation is identical, and its predefined shell variables overlap with those of Bourne. But there are two features which really mark it out from the Bourne shell, and which make life in the C shell significantly easier. These are the existence of **aliases** and the **history** facility.

## Aliases

In Unix, as elsewhere, an alias is an alternative name for something, and one used in preference to the real name. The main purpose is to make the system easier to use by reducing complex command lines to simpler shortforms, but those people used to working with DOS may also like to replace Unix command names with the more familiar DOS names.

To see if there are any aliases set for you already, type the command:

% **alias**

An alias can be given in a command line - in which case it is active for that session only - or written into the '.cshrc'. As the system runs through the commands in this file at the start of every session, your aliases will then be always there for you. Either way, the line takes the form:

% **alias** *new_name command_string*

For instance, to set an alias so that you could use a DOS-style 'dir' rather than 'ls', you would want the line:

%  **alias dir ls**

Try it now. Type it in at the prompt, then type **dir** to test it.

The 'command_string' may consist of more than just a command - it could also include optional arguments. In this case, enclose it in single quotes. Thus to give yourself a simple way to get a fully-detailed directory listing:

%  **alias ll 'ls -la'**

Or for the column-wise alternative, replace **ls -C** with  **lc** by:

%  **alias lc 'ls -C'**

Think about the way you use the system. Are there lengthy command lines that you have to type in regularly? An alias to simplify changing into a frequently used directory might be handy. If you had a sub-directory called 'textfiles', changing into it from elsewhere in your area would normally involve getting back to your home directory, then changing down from there - or giving a fuller path. This would reduce it to a few keystrokes:

%  **alias text 'cd $HOME/textfiles'**

## File Specifications and Aliases

When you type a command line that includes a simple alias like those given above, Unix expands the alias but leaves the rest of the line untouched. Any file specifications are therefore carried across. Thus:

%  **lc *.txt**

expands to:

%  **ls -C *.txt**

This gives a column-wise listing of your text files, as desired.

The situation is a little more complicated if the original command line includes a pipeline to another program. Here the file specification will be embedded in the command. The solution lies in the combination of symbols '\!*'. This typically compact and forbidding phrase translates to mean 'pick up whatever follows the alias'. (Why it works should be clearer after you have read the section on Editing Command Lines, below.) For instance, if you wanted a full directory listing, run through a screenful at a time via **pg**, your normal command line would be:

% **ls -l *filespec* | pg**

Create an 'lpg' (long, paged) alias with:

% **alias lpg 'ls -l \!* |pg'**

Typing **lpg *.pas** would then be equivalent to **ls -l *.pas |pg**.

Finally, if you are one of those who believe that computers are never user-friendly, try this:

% **alias hi 'echo clear off'**

Now try typing a cheery 'hi' to the computer and see where it gets you.

Explore the possibilities of aliases, and when you have found some that look as though they may be really useful, edit your '.cshrc' file - or create a new one if there isn't one there already - and write the alias lines into it. Next time you login, Unix will work through the '.cshrc' and set up the aliases.

## Security First

One of the problems of teaching computing is that some of the students have more brains than sense. For them, the security measures are seen as a challenge rather than a safeguard, and if they succeed in getting past them, they have to leave a marker to let people know how clever they have been. Sometimes this takes form of dropping destructive aliases into other peoples' directories. Create the alias **ls 'rm *'** and next time the victim tries to list files, they will be wiped instead!

This trouble is not very likely to happen to you, but there is a simple precaution you can take. If you put the /bin and /usr/bin at the start of your path and keep your own directories to the rear, when you give command words, the system will find and run the proper programs and never touch the booby-trapped aliases. (See below for setting the PATH in a C shell.)

## History

The history facility keeps a record of your most recent commands. This provides you with a means of finding what it was that you did that produced any particular good - or bad - results. It also makes for more efficient working - especially if you are an indifferent typist. As past commands are stored, they can be recalled and reused. And they can be edited, to correct errors or to vary their effect. The longer the command line, the more you will appreciate these repeat and edit facilities.

You should find that the facility has been set up for you already. Try it:

% **history**
13 cd
16 ls
17 alias dir ls
....
23 vi .cshrc
24 history

If it is present you will see a list of the last dozen commands, numbered in the order that they were given. If you want to see those that are further back in the record, give the number of the first and last that you want. (Or rather, take a guess at a suitable range as you are unlikely to know their numbers.) For example:

% **history 5 20**
 5 pwd
 ...
 ...
18 ls -C *.pas
19 alias ll ls -la
20 ll textfiles

If the history facility has not been turned on, set it up now by the line:

% **set history=20**

This will store the last 20 commands. Now type **date**, **ls**, **pwd** and a few other commands, to put something in the file.

With **history** active, you can recall any command in the file by typing an exclamation mark followed by either the command number (counting from login), or the start of the command string. Let's take some examples based on the first history given above. Using the 'start of command string' approach:

% **!v**
vi .cshrc

(If your system does not echo the recalled command line to the screen, then see **verbose** below, in the section on variables.)

The system has scanned back through the file and picked up the last command starting with a 'v'. If there were several starting with the same letter, and you wanted an earlier one, you would have to type enough letters to distinguish it. So, to get **ls -C \*.pas** (number 18), and not the later **ll textfiles**, you would type:

% **!ls**

There's a quickie variation on this. A double exclamation mark will repeat the last command, whatever it was.

## Adding to Recalled Command Lines

As with aliases, these abbreviations are expanded by the shell into the full commands before being sent off for processing. As a consequence, you can add parameters or pipes to the !recall and these will be incorporated into the command.

For example, suppose you have just done 'ls -la' and discovered that the directory is so full that most of it has scrolled off the screen. You should have piped it through 'pg' to get a controlled display. This will do it:

% **!! |pg**

If **ls -la** was the last job, the shell will expand the recall into **ls -la |pg**.

This quick repeat facility is of most use to those who regularly perform a limited set of commands. This is often true for programmers. Their normal flow of work is to edit a source file, attempt to compile it, edit again to correct errors, compile it again, and so on until it works. Then a test run will be incorporated into the sequence, to give an edit-compile-test cycle. A typical history might read:

```
10 vi myfile.c
11 cc myfile.c -o myfile
12 vi myfile.c
13 cc myfile.c -o myfile
14 vi myfile.c
15 cc myfile.c -o myfile
16 myfile
17 vi myfile.c
18 cc myfile.c -o myfile
19 myfile
```

With a history, the command sequence can be reduced to **!v!, !c, !m** - which must save time and typing errors.

The **command number** method works in the same way, except that you type in the number from the history file, rather than the initial characters. With that last history, you could get **vi myfile.c**, the 17th command by:

% **!17**

The numbering can also be done on a relative basis, counting back from the current command. Thus:

% **!-3**

would also give the 17th command, **vi myfile.c**, assuming that your current one is number 20.

These approaches are of limited value as it takes generally more effort to recall the history file and scan for the number, or work out how far back you gave a command, than it does to type it out afresh. It only makes sense if you want to repeat a particularly long and complex line - especially if it differs only slightly from another previous line. In that case the 'start of command' approach would not work efficiently.

## Editing Command Lines

Someone took a lot of time and trouble to build a number of clever, but not very user-friendly, editing facilities into the C shell. Two are useful and straightforward - a simple means of substituting characters to correct minor errors, and a way to slice words out of a line. If you are interested in what else is available, you can look them up in the manual entry for **csh**.

### Substitution

You can change the characters in the previous command line by writing the carat (^) followed by the characters to be removed, then a second carat and the new characters. For example:

```
% la -la myprog.*
la: Command not found   { Curses, should have typed 'ls')
% ^a^s
ls -la myprog.*               { That was what I meant }
-rw———— 1 mac   staff    5803  Nov 12 11:12 myprog.c
-rwxr-xr-x 1 mac   staff   36566  Sep 29 13:53 myprog
```

This form of substitution only works on the *previous* line. But don't forget the history list - you can always get at the ones that went before, by !recalling them. If execution of the recalled command would be time-consuming or destructive, then you can prevent execution by adding **:p** to the end of the recall instruction. The line will then by printed, but not run.

Suppose that you had recently copied a file from a distant directory into another subdirectory, with the line:

% **cp ../groupwork/reports/sales/mayjuly92.txt accounts**

After doing some work on it, you then want to copy the next quarter's report from that same place into your 'accounts' directory. A simple !recall would bring the line back, but it would also copy the file again, overwriting the changes you have just made. Writing **:p** immediately after the !recall - no space - will make it print only. The editing sequence then runs like this:

```
% !cp:p            { recall the copy line, without execution }
% cp ../groupwork/reports/sales/mayjuly92.txt accounts
% ^mayjuly^augoct        { make your changes }
cp ../groupwork/reports/sales/augoct92.txt accounts
```

**Slicing**

Each word in a command line can be referred to by number, which can be designated individually or as a range. (A word is defined as something with spaces on either side.) This allows you to copy part of a previous command into your current line. The words are designated by writing **:** followed by the word's number or one of the special symbols as shown here:

| | |
|---|---|
| **:0** | first word (the command) |
| **:n** | the *n*th word |
| **:n1-n2** | the set from word n1 to word n2 |
| **:^** | second word (first argument or parameter) |
| **:$** | last word |
| **:*** | all the words following the command |

Let's take some examples based on the line: **ls -ls *.txt |pg**

| Code | Result | |
|---|---|---|
| **:0** | ls | first word (command) |
| **:^** or **:1** | -la | second word (first argument) |
| **:0-2** | ls -la *.tx | words 0 to 2 |
| **:$** or **:3** | |pg | fourth and last word |
| **:*** | -la |pg | all the words after 'ls' |

To use these in practice, we also have to specify the line that we are cutting from. Let's carry on from that long command line we had earlier. Having copied the file into the 'accounts' directory, we now want to move into it to work there.

**cp ../groupwork/reports/sales/augoct92.txt accounts**

**% cd !cp:$**          { the last word only }
cd accounts

Notice that the word designator follows immediately after the !recall. **!cp :$** (with a space) would not work.

Words can be sliced out of the **current line** in the same way. This may sound slightly pointless but cast your mind back to the aliases. There you met the expression '\!*'. The single exclamation mark refers to the current line, and the asterisk to all the words that follow the command. (The backslash in front of the exclamation mark stops the shell from expanding it within the alias line.)

# Predefined Variables

Some of these are directly equivalent to the shell parameters of Bourne; others are specific to the C shell. What follows is not a complete list, but a selection of the ones I find are most useful. **set** will tell you the current settings of your shell variables. Try it:

```
$ set
LOGTTY  /dev/tty1a
argv    ()
curterm 1a
history 50
home    /u/staff/mac
path    (/bin /etc /usr/bin /usr/local/bin bin/ . )
prompt  [1a]mac[!]->
shell   /bin/csh
status  0
```

## echo - Repeat Command Lines

If turned on, this causes command lines - from the prompt or from scripts - to be echoed to the screen before execution. It is set by invoking the C shell with the command **csh -x**.

## home - Login Directory

This is equivalent to the Bourne parameter HOME, and contains the name of your home directory. It is set by the system at login, and shouldn't be changed.

The tilde (~) is a handy shortform for the expression '$HOME'. This line, for example, would copy a file from '/tmp' to your 'letters' sub-directory, wherever you where in the system at the time.

   % **cp /tmp/oct1992.txt ~/letters**

## ignoreeof - EOF marker Active

When you are running a program, [Ctrl]-[D] acts as an end of file (eof) marker. You might type it, for instance to mark the end of the input from the keyboard. If the **ignoreeof** variable is set to 'off', [Ctrl]-[D] will close down a shell, or log you out if you are in your main shell. This may be convenient, but if you find that you are logging yourself out accidentally with [Ctrl]-[D], then set this variable to 'on' with:

   **set ignoreof = TRUE**

## mail - Path to the Mailbox

This is an environment variable, and equivalent to Bourne's MAIL. It holds the path to your mailbox on the system. Echo it to the screen and you should see something like:

   **mail=/usr/spool/mail/fred**

## path - Directories to Search

This is identical to the Bourne PATH. Note that with this, as with other key environmental variables, the normal **set** command does not work. You must instead use **setenv**, in the form:

    setenv PATH /bin:/usr/bin:.

## prompt - Input Prompt String

Where the Bourne shell has two prompt - PS1 for the main prompt and PS2 where additional input is required - the C shell has only the one. The default is %, or # for the superuser, but system administrators often like to provide something a little more interesting for their users. Try this, but inserting your own name in place of mine:

    % set prompt = 'mac[\!]->'
    mac[25]->

The '!' in the prompt is expanded into the current event number. This isn't just a visible reminder of how many things you have done during the session - gratifying though that may be - it also permits a more effective use of the history list. When you are giving a command line that you know you may well want to use later, make a note of its event number from the prompt. You can then recall it by number when you want it.

## status - Result of Last Command

This is equivalent to Bourne's **?**, and returns the exit status of the last command. Built-in commands all return values of 1, if they fail, and 0 if successfully carried out. If a program is aborted, octal 200 (128 denary) is added to its exit status.

## verbose - Echo !Recalled Commands

If turned on, this echoes the command lines recalled from the history list. Set it by starting the C shell with the variation **csh -v**.

# Chapter 11

# Finding Files

It is alarmingly easy to lose track of files, unless you are highly organised in your directory structures and choice of filenames. Even the best Unix users have bad days when they cannot remember a filename or its directory, and at times like that, any help in locating files is welcome. Fortunately Unix comes equipped with a number of utilities that can tackle the problem from several directions. There are two main tools. **find** offers a very sophisticated search facility, and is ideal if you know the name, but not the location; **grep** will let you find a text file on the basis of key words or phrases. Other utilities can also be pressed into service for tracking down lost items. **file** is a key one in this category, in that it helps to identify the contents of directories. We will start with that.

## file - Find the Type of a File

This is the enhanced alternative to **ls**, first covered briefly in Chapter 5. As well as listing files, it examines them and makes an educated guess at their nature. Some have a *magic number* written into them, which identifies their type. Some don't, but **file** has other tricks up its sleeve. With ASCII files, it scans the first 512 characters and tries to identify the programming language. **file** is generally right, though there's no guarantee.

Unlike **ls**, this command must be given a file name, wildcard expression or a directory name. You can find out about an individual file:

```
$ file sept27
sept27:      ascii text
```

It doesn't tell me much, but at least I know whether to read it or run it.

115

Use the * wildcard to see what sort of things you have in a directory:

```
$ file *
BROKERS:           ascii text
BROKERS.idx:       data
Mail:              directory
P:                 commands text
add.c:             c program text
brokerlist:        ascii text
brokers:           unix-rt ldp
bubble:            Microsoft a.out separate pure segmented
word-swapped not-stripped 386 executable
cert.txt:          ascii text
pascal:            directory
sortroutines:      commands text
strings:           commands text
sum.c:             c program text
wp.back.up:        ascii text
```

This particular directory is something of a dump for odds and ends, but at least it demonstrates some of the types that are recognised by **file**. These include directories (which are also files as far as Unix is concerned), executable programs, data files, plain ascii text, text files for most programming languages and shell scripts (labelled 'commands text').

**file** will look into a sub-directory - or a distant directory, identified by its path. The command usage is subtly different from that of **ls**. Where **ls accounts** would list those in the 'accounts' directory, **file accounts** will simply give you:

```
accounts    directory
```

To get it to look beyond this and tell you what's inside, you must also include a file specification:

```
$ file accounts/b*
bill27may    ascii text
buyers.idx   data
...
```

This will give you the types of all the files starting with 'b' in the accounts sub-directory.

## file Options

### -f namefile

Use this where you will regularly want to check a certain set of files. It will save typing the file specifications each time. The *namefile* is a file containing the names - with wildcards if wanted - of the files to be type checked.

### -m magicfile

This is for advanced users only. The *magic number* referred to above is a code, written into some types of files by the system. The standard lookup table, to translate these codes into words, is stored in the file '/etc/magic'. If you want to extend the facility to include your own type codes, you will have to take a copy of this and add your at the end. You could then use this option to make it work from your 'magicfile'.

Have a look at '/etc/magic' before you contemplate embarking on this yourself. It is a lengthy and complex file.

## find - Locate a File

This sounds simple enough, but it is one of the more powerful commands, and in Unix power and simplicity rarely go together. Essentially it finds files that match certain conditions, and it may then go on to perform actions if matching files are present. The search runs through all the sub-directories below the start point, and the conditions can be name, size, type or time since last accessed - amongst others. Combine this with a remove or copy command and you have a very useful file management utility.

The basic shape of the command is:

> find *start_of_path options & arguments action*

There is variation, as not all options take arguments, you will often use more than one option at a time, and it is not necessary to specify an action.

## find Options

**-print** by itself has no effect. Give it after a file-finding options and it will make **find** print the names of those that match. The names will be given with their full paths - and hence their locations. If you want a permanent copy of the output for later reference, >redirect it into a file, or add a **tee** pipe fitting to get both immediate screen output and a file.

**-name** *filename* must be the easiest and the most useful of the **find** variations. Use it to track down lost files. The option is followed by a filename or wildcard expression. Start looking somewhere above the directory in which you believe the file to be - which means, if you haven't got a clue, go to your home directory. The specification for the start_of_path can then be a simple dot (.) - meaning the current directory. Give the filename in full if you know it and want only that file. And don't forget the **-print** to get the feedback.

For example, to find the file 'urgent.memo' that you wrote last week and forgot to mail:

```
$ cd                          { go to home directory }
$ find . -name urgent.memo -print
/usr/staff/john/jobs/urgent.memo
```

There it is, in John's 'jobs' directory. If John had got the name wrong, so that it could not be found, the **find** command would have given no feedback - not even a 'Not found' message.

Where you are unsure of the name, or want to track down a set of related files, you can use wildcard expressions. These must be enclosed in quotes so that the expression is passed through the shell to **find**, before it is expanded.

Suppose that John was looking for the minutes of a meeting held in July, and could remember only that the name would have started with 'jul' or 'july'. He might have tried this:

118

**$ find . -name 'jul*' -print**
/usr/staff/john/sales/jul15.rpt
/usr/staff/john/sales/jul25.memo
/usr/staff/john/accounts/jul7invs.sum
/usr/staff/john/misc/jul30dti.mins
/usr/staff/john/personal/julie.invite

The **find** has turned up a promising file in the 'misc' directory. That will be worth closer inspection. It has also turned up an invitation from Julie, which John may also have forgotten about!

**$ find . -name '*.pas' -print |tee pasfiles**
.....
.....

This time the command will produce a list of all the Pascal source files. The **|tee** pipeline splits the output, giving a screen display and storing a permanent record of the list in 'pasfiles'.

The **find -name** is so handy that it is worth creating an alias (if you work in a C or Korn shell) to make it easier to use. A suitable alias would be:

**alias fnd find . -name '\!*' -print**

The '\!*' expression carries your file specification through to the full command line. To use it, you would go to a suitable point on the directory tree - it runs from the current directory - and give the command in the form:

**fnd *filename*.**

**-type** finds files of a given type, with the types specified by the code letters:

| | |
|---|---|
| b | block special |
| c | character special |
| d | directory |
| p | pipe |
| f | plain file |

You can probably forget about 'block' and 'character' files - these are external devices, and the 'pipe' files are for advanced users. However, the other two are immediately useful.

Give **find** with the 'd' option to see your directory structure. Here's what I get, running it from my home directory:

```
$ find . -type d -print
/usr/staff/mac
/usr/staff/mac/basic
/usr/staff/mac/pascal
/usr/staff/mac/.iosmail
/usr/staff/mac/progassigns
/usr/staff/mac/qmassigns
/usr/staff/mac/c
/usr/staff/mac/Mail
/usr/staff/mac/UAP
/usr/staff/mac/UAP/PRINT
/usr/staff/mac/example
/usr/staff/mac/micropro
```

**-atime -ctime** are very similar options, and will match any files that were last accessed (**-atime**) or changed (**-ctime**) on a given day. The day is specified by number, counting back from today, with today being 0. The **-ctime** option is probably used more than the other. A typical use for it is to find those files that have been changed during the day and that therefore should be copied to the backup tape overnight. The command line to find today's files would be:

```
$find . -ctime 0 -print
```

**-exec** *command* solves the problem of what to do with files after you have found them. It passes each located file across to the following *command*. This can be any suitable file-processing operation, and is given in its normal form, except that a pair of closed parentheses {} replace the file argument and the command must be ended by an escaped semi-colon \;. For example, to remove all your backup files - from all your directories - go to your home directory and run this:

```
$ find . -name '*.bak' -exec rm {} \;
```

It's not always plain sailing. You might reasonably expect the following line to copy those files that have been changed today across into directory called 'backup'.

**$ find . -ctime 0 -exec cp {} backup \;**

This will give you more than you bargained for! As the current directory and any sub-directories are also files to Unix, and as they are updated when any of their files are changed, the **find** command also matches those. As a result, all their component files are copied across to 'backup' as well. There is a solution to this problem, but it is takes a shell script, rather than just a tweak to the command line. In case you are interested, here's one way to tackle it.

```
{ shell script, perhaps called 'filebak' }
find . -ctime 0 -print | while read found
do
if test -d $found
then
echo Directory
elif test -f $found
then
cp $found backup
fi
done
```

Briefly, what is happening here is this. The output from the **find** is piped across to the 'while' routine. Each file in turn is captured by the variable 'found'. It is then tested to see if it is a directory or a proper file, and only the latter are copied into the 'backup' directory. If you want to know more about the shell structures used in this script, turn to Chapter 16.

## Compound Expressions

What follows is not specific to **find**, but applies in any situation where you want to pass an AND/OR expression through the shell to a command. There are two operators:

| | | |
|---|---|---|
| **-o** | OR | TRUE if either or both tests are true |
| **!** | NOT | reverse TRUE and FALSE |

AND, meaning 'TRUE only if both tests are true' has no operator, but is assumed if there are two test in the expression, with no '-o' linking them

The catch is that compound tests must be enclosed in () brackets and that brackets have a special meaning to the shell. To pass them through to the command, they must be escaped by \ backslash.

For example, you are looking for a file which you think you either called 'annual.rpt' or 'end_of_year.doc'. Rather than do two separate searches, you can join the alternative tests with an OR (**-o**), enclosed in brackets. The **find** command is then:

```
$ find . \( -name annual.rpt -o -name end_of_year.doc \) -print
/usr/staff/bill/text/old/annual.rpt
/usr/staff/bill/text/backup/end_of_year.doc
```

Note that the **-name** option is specified for each test.

In this example, the **find** has turned up copies of the file under each of the alternative names. This is not an unusual experience. A back-up copy made towards the end of a long session is quite easy to forget, and programmers will often generate many files holding variations of the same program, as they refine and embellish their original draft. Rummaging through the cupboards and throwing away unwanted clutter every now and then makes for a tidy house. Extend the good housekeeping to your Unix directories.

## grep - Search Files for Text Strings

**grep** - the 'general regular expression pattern matcher' - searches through files and displays any lines that contain the given string. It can be used in several valuable ways. Its primary purpose is to search database files - i.e those where each line contains one record, subdivided into fields. You give it a value to be looked for, and it will produce a set of records that contain a matching string. But its use is by no means restricted to database. It provides a quick way of locating text within any text file. If the displayed line has all the data you need, then no further action is needed, and if not, at least you know where to start looking when you load the file into **vi** or whatever editor. Finally - and the reason why I have included it in this chapter - you can use it to find files where you have forgotten the filenames but can remember a key word or phrase.

At its simplest, **grep** takes the form:

**grep *expression filename***

The *expression* can be a simple string - either a single word or a phrase enclosed in quotes, or may contain special characters that influence the nature of the search. Let's start with simple strings. For example, you want to send some mail to Fiona, but do not know her user name. That information is contained in the '/etc/passwd' file. All users have read access to this - the actual passwords are either written there in an encoded version, or stored elsewhere, depending upon the system. You can't write to the file, delete it or change it in any way - only the superuser has that kind of access to /etc/passwd - but read access is all you need for **grep**. This command will scan the file and display the line containing 'Fiona':

```
$ grep Fiona /etc/passwd
fp295:*:295:102:Fiona Pearce,admin:/u/staff/admin/fiona:/bin/sh
```

This tells us that her user name is 'fp295' - it is fairly common practice to create user names from initials and user numbers. At the far right of the line you can see her home directory and login shell. This system uses the Bourne shell - activated by **/bin/sh** at login.

## Wildcards

As elsewhere in Unix, you can replace a single filename with a wildcard expression. And this is how you can find files when you have forgotten their names, but can remember something of what they contained. The wildcard expression will extend the search over a set of files. All you need to do is give a key string that will pick up the right file.

Suppose that you have had a reply to a memo that you sent to the management - the one about the car parking arrangements. They want to discuss your ideas in depth, so you had best dig out your file copy. But what was it called? You haven't a clue, but can clearly recall using the phrase 'laudably democratic'. It's not an expression you often use and should be an excellent key. Your command line then runs:

**$ grep 'laudably democratic ' ***
meters: be laudably democratic to allocate a slot to your secretary

Now you remember that you called the file 'meters' as you had been forced to park on those for the previous week.

Programmers may find **grep** useful for tracking down functions and commands in existing programs, either to copy them into the current program, or to check on their usage. I'm having trouble with the 'strcmp' function in my new C program, and the **man** entry for it is not clear. Where and how have I used in successfully in the past?

**$ grep strcmp *.c**
lockup.c:      if (strcmp(outfile, "temp.$$$") == 0)
prettyc.c:            found = strcmp(check,keyword[loop++]);
treedir.c:      case 1:  if (strcmp(n,branch->name) < 0)
treedir.c:      case 2:  if (strcmp(e,branch->date) < 0)

That turns up examples in three different programs. One of those should give me the help I need.

## grep Options

**-i** With this set, **grep ignores** the distinction between capitals and lower case. For example, to find Simon's user name, I could use this:

**$ grep -i simon /etc/passwd**
eagle:*:236:499:Simon Row,NDCS1:/u/student/dip1/eagle:/bin/csh
kiwi:*:240:499:simon brown,NDCS1:/u/student/dip1/kiwi:/bin/csh
wasp:*:350:108:SIMON GREEN,FCIT:/u/student/fcit/wasp:/bin/csh

(We have an idiosyncratic approach to user names on our system.) The key word for **grep** could equally well have been 'SIMON', or 'Simon'. The result would have been the same.

**-c** Will **count** lines. With this option set, **grep** suppresses the display of lines and tells you only how many contained matching strings. You can use it to find how many records in a database hold a particular value. For example, how many First Year Diploma students do we have? They are identified by 'dip1' in their /etc/passwd entries.

```
$ grep -c dip1 /etc/passwd
38
```

The answer is a simple number. If the search extends across more than one file, then each filename is listed, with a count value at the end. In which C programs can I find examples of the 'strcat' function?

```
$ grep -c strcat *.c
bsearch.c:0
cclean.c:0
...
...
test.c:0
tidyup.c:4
tree.c:0
treedir.c:4
wpr.c:3
```

**-l** This option suppresses the display of **lines** containing the matched expression. At the simplest, you can use it where you are only interested in the matching files, and not in the details of the containing lines - in which Pascal programs, for example, have I used 'REWRITE'?

```
$ grep -l REWRITE *.pas
linker.pas
print.pas
stocktest.pas
upd.pas
update.pas
```

At a more advanced level, you can use it to get filenames to pass on to command that is piped onto the end of the **grep**.

**-n** Asks **grep** to show line **numbers.** I suspect that this option is mainly intended for use with **ed,** the old line-based text editor, but it still has some value. As it will give you the line as well as the file, it pinpoints the location of items and can speed up later editing.

```
$ grep -n strcmp *.c
lockup.c:84:      if (strcmp(outfile, "temp.$$$") == 0)
prettyc.c:62:          found = strcmp(check,keyword[loop++]);
treedir.c:39:     case 1:  if (strcmp(n,branch->name) < 0)
treedir.c:40:     case 2:  if (strcmp(e,branch->date) < 0)
```

**-f** *filename* Takes the expression from a file. This is handy if you are using the same complex expression frequently. Write it into a file, then give the filename instead of the search string.

Suppose, for example, that you were afflicted by the unfortunate habit of writing 'at this moment in time' when you really mean 'now'. It is something that you do unconsciously, so you have to check your texts from time to time to remove it. Try this. Create a file called 'now', consisting of the line:

**'at this moment in time'**      { including the quotes }

You can then scan your text files for this clumsy Americanism by the command:

**$ grep -f now *.txt**

**-v** Reverses the match. The effect is to output every line in the specified files except those that match the pattern. Use with care. You could get more than you anticipated.

## grep Patterns

**grep**'s special characters allow you to construct patterns containing wildcards, instead of a simple target string. They can also specify, to a limited extent, whereabouts in the lines to search for a matching string.

The main **wildcard** here is . (dot), which can stand for any single character.

### $ grep 'Sm.th' /etc/passwd

This would find any occurrence of 'Smith', 'Smyth' or 'Smythe' - there's no need to give a wildcard for that final 'e' as **grep** finds partial and whole word matches.

The asterisk (*) - the normal shell wildcard - serves a different purpose here. In **grep** it is a repeater. Write this after a character to match any number of repetitions of that character. Its most common use is in conjunction with dot, where the pair act like the normal shell wildcard.

### $ grep 'John R.*son' namelist

This will find John Robertson, John Robinson, John Robson or any other John whose surname starts with 'R' and ends with 'son'.

The '.*' combination can also act as an AND, linking two patterns. For example, if you had a staff database which held, amongst other things, people's current age and their birthday - and they were stored in that order - you check to see who had a fortieth coming up in a given month by a command like this:

### $ grep '39.*Dec' staff.data

Alternative characters, or a range of possibles, can be given in [ ] (square brackets). The search can be inverted - i.e. match everything except the given set of characters - by writing a caret (^) just inside the bracket.

### $ grep 'ls -[lt]' script.sh    { alternatives }
### $ grep 'num[1-4]' myprog.pas    { range of possibles }
### $ grep '[^sf]printf' myprog.c    { not 's' or 'f' at the start }

The first of these would match 'ls -l' and 'ls -t' in the shell script, but ignore 'ls -a', 'ls -F' and other variations. The second find the variables 'num1', 'num2', 'num3' and/or 'num4' in the Pascal program. With the third, **grep** would pass over lines containing 'sprintf' and 'fprintf', matching only the 'printf' lines in the C program.

## Position

The caret (^) also has a second and quite different effect. If it is placed at the beginning of the string, it specifies that the match is to be sought at the beginnings of lines. Similarly, a dollar sign ($) at the end of a string points **grep** to the ends of lines.

```
$ grep '^do' *.c      { line starts with 'do' }
$ grep 'pg$' *        { line ends with 'pg' }
```

By fixing the position, the '^do' expression will focus on the start of 'do .. while' loops in the C programs, but ignore (most) occurrences of 'do' in print lines or variable names - though it would still pick up lines such as 'done = TRUE;'. The 'pg$' search, presumably aimed at shell scripts, would likewise pass over those lines that started with 'pg' or used it as an intermediate pipe.

### Restoring Normal Service

If you looking for one of these symbols - as a normal characters, remove its special significance by prefixing it with the backslash (\).

```
$ grep '\^' *.pas
```

Now you can find a Pascal program that uses pointers. (A type of variable marked by a caret.)

## Redirection

Don't forget that the output from any command can be redirected to a file, or sent off for further processing through a pipe. This is particularly useful with **find** and **grep**. Having tracked down the matching files, or the matching lines within files, you can then do something with them directly, rather than just view them on the screen.

```
$ grep alevel /etc/passwd >alevel.list
```

This command would send the entries for the A level students to file, for later reference.

## grep in Pipes

**grep** can be a convenient way of filtering the output from a command. Where you are going to get more than you really want, add a **grep** pipe to the end of the line to focus on that part of the output which really interests you. For example, you want to know if Freddie is logged in, but there are a lot of users on the system. Rather than having to scan a lengthy output, you can **get grep** to do it for you:

```
$ who |grep freddie
freddie   tty14 Nov 18 10:49
```

Yes, he's there and has been working since 10:49.

## grep Variations - egrep and fgrep

These two utilities are almost identical to **grep** but offer additional flexibility in the types of expressions that can be used. In different ways, each will allow you to specify more than one pattern in your search expression. With **egrep** you can build OR expressions, and with **fgrep** you can give a whole set of alternative patterns. The normal **grep** options work with them both.

In **egrep**, each pattern should be enclosed in (brackets), and separated by a broken vertical bar (|) or a newline, with the whole expression enclosed in quotes. The bar is the obvious choice, but if you want to use a newline, precede it with the backslash. If you don't, Unix will think that you have finished the command line as soon as you press [Enter] - and then complain that it is incomplete.

These will both have the same effect of picking out any lines that contain either 'John' or 'Jane'.

```
$ egrep '(John) | (Jane)' stafflist
$ egrep '(John) \
(Jane)' stafflist
```

**fgrep** will only work with fixed strings - no wildcards here. As this makes it a simpler routine, it runs faster than the standard **grep**. (On a decent system, you are unlikely to notice the difference unless you are searching through large directories stuffed with files.) Though the string patterns must be fixed, you can have any number of them in the search list. The separator here must be a newline (backslash then [Enter]), and the whole set must be enclosed in quotes.

```
$ fgrep 'May \
June \
July \
August \
September' *.memo
```

Where you have a set of text items that you want to search for regularly, write them into a file, and use the **-f** option. Some system administrators use this method to scan the mailboxes for unacceptable words - including any references to the system administrator!

```
$ fgrep -f censor /usr/spool/mail/*
```

**grep** is a handy tool, and one that we shall use later. Meanwhile, as we have started to slice items out of files, let's look further into the cut and paste facilities in Unix.

# Chapter 12

# Text File Processing

The sort of 'text file processing' that we are looking at here is not 'processing' in the sense of word processing or otherwise preparing text for publication. There are Unix utilities that will do that, but they are not easy to use. I suspect that nowadays, most users who want good-looking printed output, will either turn to a specialised word-processing application on their Unix system, or switch to a PC or an Apple Mac and run their text through a desk-top publishing package. If these options are not available to you, and you still want to control the type styles and layout, then the System V Unix software does include a very sophisticated utility that will do it. It's called **nroff**, and you can read all about it in the User's Reference Manual.

What we will be covering in this chapter are those simpler, but useful commands that will process text files either as wholes or in large chunks. The more detailed 'cut and paste' utilities will be dealt with in the next chapter.

### cat - Concatenate and Display Files

You met this first in Chapter 2, where we used it to send files to the screen, and again in Chapter 6, where it was used, along with the redirector, to create files. These could be completely new, capturing input from the keyboard, or be made up from existing files, concatenated together. To summarise those three ways of using **cat**:

| | |
|---|---|
| **cat *files*** | { display files on screen } |
| **cat *files* > *newfile*** | { join files to make new one } |
| **cat *files* >> *oldfile*** | { append files to end of old file } |
| **cat > *newfile*** | { redirect input to a file } |

131

In these, *'files'* can be one or any number of separate files, though as they are run together without any break, you would rarely **cat** more than one at a time to the screen.

## cat Options

### -v Make Non-printing Characters Visible

The screen can only handle safely the letters, digits and symbols that make up the core of the ASCII set (characters 32 to 126). Characters outside this range will have special meanings, that vary from terminal to terminal. Character 7 will make the terminal 'beep', another will clear the screen, others will move the cursor, turn on the highlight, or even turn off the terminal!

There are no problems as long as you are working with plain text, but a file may contain other characters. If it was word-processed, it may have codes to control the printer - selecting fonts, setting line spacing, margins and the like. If it is a data file, then the numbers may be in machine format, rather than as strings of digits. Send files like this to the screen with a simple **cat** and the results will be unpredictable. Use the **-v** option and the non-printing characters will be made visible in the form ^C. The 'C' refers to the key which, if you pressed it, while holding [Ctrl], would create that character. Thus the [Ctrl]-[Z] (end of file) character would show up with **cat -v** as ^Z.

The simple print control characters - tab, carriage return and line feed - are processed as normal even with the **-v** option on.

**-s Suppresses** error messages. If you tell **cat** to print a file and it can't find it, then **cat** will tell you so. This is all well and good most of the time, but within a shell program you might prefer to suppress the error message.

**-e** Print **End of Line** Marker. This option can only be used in combination with **-v**. It puts a '$' at the end of each line. It will therefore show up trailing spaces and help to identify those logical lines that occupy more than one line on the screen.

**cat** works well for displaying small files, but as it pours text through in a continual stream, it is not convenient for anything that runs to more than one screen. For larger files, you are better off with **pg**, which we will get to in a moment, or **head** or **tail**.

## head - Display the Start of a File

**head** is a handy, but often over-looked, little utility. It displays the top end - normally the first 10 lines - of a file. I find it useful for checking that a file really is the one I think it is, or that a cut and paste operation has had the desired effect. In either case you often only need to see a few lines to be sure.

Check it out with any lengthy file. If you want to create one quickly, redirect the listing from a big directory, like 'bin', into a file.

```
$ ls /bin >binlist
$ head binlist
STTY
[
acctcom
adb
ar
as
asm
auths
basename
bfs
```

If 10 lines, the default setting, is too many or too few for you, set the number of lines you want:

```
$ head -5 binlist
STTY
[
acctcom
adb
ar
```

## tail - Display the End of a File

**tail** solves the big file problem from the other end, though this command has a little more too it. The basic command takes the same form.

```
$ tail binlist
whodo
write
wtty
x286emul
xbackup
xdump
xdumpdir
xrestor
xrestore
yes
```

The default display is of the last 10 lines, but the starting place can be changed. You can either count from the top of the file, indicated by **+n**, or from the bottom (**-n**), where 'n' is the number of lines. In either case, **tail** will display to the end of the file. There is no means of specifying an earlier end. For example:

```
$ tail +50 myprog.c
$ tail -5 herprog.c
```

The first starts at line 50, the second 5 lines from the end.

By default **tail** works in lines, but this can be in characters - indicated by **c** option - or blocks of 512 characters (**b**). The letter must be written after the +/- start place specifier. For example:

```
$ tail -100 c letter.text
$ tail +3 b bigfile.data
```

This will give you the last 100 characters of 'letter.txt' and the third and subsequent blocks of 'bigfile.data'.

Note that when a file is tailed, the relevant part is stored in a buffer of limited size, and very long tails can be cut short.

## **pg** - View a File by Pages

So far we have used **pg** simply for reading through a file one page at a time, and only noted a couple of commands - **h** to call up Help, and **q** to Quit. There is rather more to **pg** than that. **pg** is a fully fledged file viewing utility. With it you can move backwards and forwards through a file, leap to a specified place, search for a string of text or switch between several files. The controls for this work at two levels. The command line options set the basic nature of the viewing environment, and inputs while **pg** is running handle the switch and search facilities.

## **pg** Command Line Options

*-number* selects how many lines to display at a time. The default is one less than the screen height. This option should not be confused with ...

*+number,* which specifies the line at which to start viewing. e.g.

> **$ pg +50 -20 longfile**

This pages through 'longfile', 20 lines at a time, starting at line 50.

*+/pattern/* starts the viewing at the first line containing a matching string. The *pattern* follows the same rules as in **grep**. This is handy. Having used **grep** to locate a text item, you can then view it in context with **pg**. I know I wrote a string to number conversion function in one of my Pascal programs. Where is it and what does it look like? I think I called it 'str_to_num' or something similar:

```
$ grep 'str.*num' *.pas    {starts with 'str' ends with 'num'}
grep 'str.*num' *.pas
calc.pas:function str_num(str:string; base:integer):integer;
calc.pas:  str_num := num;
calc.pas:  value := str_num(s,b);
```

I now know that it is present in 'calc.pas', but that is a long program. I can leap direct to the relevant section and display 15 lines, which should be enough, with the **pg** command line:

**$ pg -15 +/str_num/ calc.pas**

```
function str_num(str:string; base:integer):integer;
var
loop,digit:integer;

begin
num:= 0;
for loop := 1 to 8 do
if (str[loop] >= '0') and (str[loop] <= 'F')
then begin
        if (str[loop] <= '9')
        then digit := ord(str[loop]) - 48;
        else digit := ord(str[loop]) - 55;
        num := num * base + digit;
    end;
str_num := num;
:
```

**-c clears** the screen before printing each new page, rather than scrolling up from the bottom.

**-p** *string* defines a new **prompt** to replace the bare ':'. The current page number can be worked into the prompt by the special combination '%d'. For really smart paging, use this in conjunction with ...

**-s,** (short for '**standout**') which highlights the prompt and any messages. e.g.

**$ pg -p 'Page %d :' -s mytext**

This will give you a bright, clear page number at the bottom of the screen, and knowing that number can be useful.

## pg Internal Controls

While **pg** is sending text to the screen, **[Ctrl]-[D]**, **[Del]** or **[^]** will stop the flow and bring up the **pg** prompt. All the other commands are given in response to that prompt. They fall into three groups.

## Movement

This can be either absolute or relative, and is usually measured in pages. Give a number by itself to leap to a chosen page. Put a + or - in front to move forwards or backwards a set number of pages. If you want to move by lines, rather than pages, write '1' (letter L) after the number. For example:

| | |
|---|---|
| **: 3** | { go to page 3 } |
| **: 25 l** | { display from line 25 onwards } |
| **: +2** | { skip 2 pages forward } |
| **: -10 l** | { scroll back 10 lines } |

There are two other movement commands. Use **.** (dot) to redisplay the current page, and **$** to leap to the last windowful. Note that this may have unexpected results if you are using **pg** in a pipe.

## Search

The internal search uses the same pattern formats (the **ed/grep** standards) as the command line option. A simple search for the next occurrence of the word 'function', for instance, would take the form:

### : /function/

The nature of the operation can be controlled in three ways. You can search backwards by replacing the /slashes/ with ?question marks?. You can jump to a particular occurrence if a string by writing a number at the start of the command. Finally, you can tack an **m** to the end to set the display so that the line containing the matching string is at the middle of the screen, or a **b** to place it at the bottom.

| | |
|---|---|
| **: 2/function/** | { go to the 2nd match, from the current page } |
| **: ?'char c'?** | { go back and find 'char c' } |
| **: /meeting/ m** | { find 'meeting' and display in mid-screen } |

## File Handling

s *filename* saves the current file. This is not as pointless as it may sound. If you are using **pg** in a pipe, this gives you the option of retaining data that would be otherwise only sent to the screen. If you are using it to scan a set of old files, then this option lets you make a copy as you work your way through.

If you have started **pg** with a list of files, you can close down the current file and jump on or back to a different one. Note that you are working by their position in the list of files, not the filenames. The commands take the form of a number followed by **n** for 'next' or **p** for 'previous'. Suppose that you had started with the command line:

### $ pg chap1.txt chap2.txt chap3.txt chap4.txt chap5.txt

You have paged through to 'chap3.txt', each file coming into view as the previous ends. You now want to view a different file.

> **: 2p**     { go back 2, to 'chap1.txt' }
> **: 1n**     { go on to next file, jumping out of the current one }

## split - Split a File

This takes a file and sub-divides it into a set of files of fixed length. (The original file stays intact.) This is a crude but quick way to reduce a large file to manageable chunks.

The new files are labelled with a two-letter appendage to their name, starting with **aa** and going up to **zz**. If you accept the default settings, the output files will be called 'xaa', 'xab', 'xac', etc, and will be 1000 lines long. The length and the new filenames can be easily set.

For example, to divide 'bigprog.lst', a sizable error report produced when trying to compile a Cobol program, into 40-line segments whose names start with 'bigbit', you would use the line:

### $ **split -40 bigprog.lst bigbit**

This gives you 'bigbitaa', bigbitab', 'bigbitac' and the like. You can now run these out to the printer, leaving deep bottom margins for note-writing:

### $ **lp bigbit***

(Your system may well use an alternative to **lp**, designed to send output to a specific printer.)

This simple division by length is rarely of much practical use. It is generally more useful to divide into logical sections, based on content. For that you need **csplit**.

## **csplit** - Spilt Files by Context

This splits files on the basis of key words - or rather, **grep** style expressions that generate key words or phrases. It can also perform a simpler split based on line count, or a combination of the two. Like **split** it produces a set of files where the names share a common base, though here the part-identifiers are numbers not letters. By default, the part files are named 'xx00', 'xx01', 'xx02', etc. The essential form of the command is:

### **csplit [options]** *source_file key1 key2 ...*

The file is split so that the first of the resulting files runs from the start to the line before the first key, and each key word is in the first line of a new section. Obviously, to split a file successfully by key words, you need to know where the words are. If you have to read the text to find out where to split, you may as well use the block write facilities of **vi** or of your word-processor. In practice, most **csplit**s would be based on section headings in text files or procedure labels in programs.

To see how it works, let's take this summary of a recent Government White Paper. (Write your own version with **vi** - it will be good practice with the yank and paste facilities.)

139

```
woffle
woffle
woffle
Proposals
blah
blah
blah
blah
Summary
rhubarb
rhubarb
rhubarb
rhubarb

$ csplit paper /Proposals/ /Summary/
21
30
40
```

Note that the key expressions are each enclosed in /slashes/. As we have given no base filenames, the default 'xx..' forms are used. The numbers that are printed at the end of the operation, are the character counts for each of the new files.

```
$ cat xx00
woffle
woffle
woffle
$ cat xx01
Proposals                        { the first key word }
blah
blah
blah
blah
$ cat xx02
Summary
rhubarb
rhubarb
rhubarb
rhubarb
```

## csplit Options

There are three options, which can be used alone or in any combination.

**-s Suppresses** the character count display on completion;
**-k Keeps** the files created up to that point if an error causes the command to stop. These would normally be wiped as **csplit** takes an all-or-nothing approach.
**-f** *name* sets a basename for the new files.

Test them. Give a filename, and write an error into the line so that the command will fail.

```
$ csplit -k -f cutting paper /Proposals/ /Conclusion/
21
/Conclusion/ - out of range
70
```

That 'out of range' error tells us that **csplit** reached the end of the file without finding a match for the string. If you check the new files, you will see that the second includes everything from 'Proposals' to the end.

```
$ cat cutting01
Proposals
blah
....
rhubarb
rhubarb
```

## csplit Arguments

So far we have only used simple string expressions to split the file, but there are three other possibilities here.

Enclose the string in %percent% signs and **csplit** does not write the section that is ended by that expression.

```
$ csplit paper /Proposals/ %Summary%
```

141

This will give you two files - the first few lines, up to 'Proposals', and the last section from 'Summary' onwards.

According to the Manual, **csplit** can take two types of numeric argument. In theory, if you give a **number**, by itself, that will split off a file containing that number of lines, starting from the current position; while a number enclosed in {parentheses} will repeat the previous argument for that number of times:

### $ csplit -k bigfile 50 {100}

This should split 'bigfile' into 50 line segments. (The '-k' option ensures that if there are less than 100 segments, those that have been created are kept when the command terminates.)

In practice, on the (SCO System V) installation that I work with, **csplit** behaves in a different way - the **man** entry notwithstanding. The {number} arguments are simply ignored, while plain numbers are treated as absolute line references. Thus:

### $ csplit bigfile 50

splits the file into two segments; the first running from line 1 to 49, the second from line 50 onwards.

### $ csplit bigfile 50 150 300

This would split the file into 4 segments, containing lines 1-49, 50-149, 150-299 and 300 to the end. Test yours carefully before using this command in earnest.

## csplit in Pipes

With most commands, the input filename is omitted when the command is used in a pipeline. With **csplit**, you must write a dash in place of the filename.

## wc - Word Counter

This utility is probably of most use to journalist and students - or anyone else who gets paid or marked by the word! It will tell you the number of lines, words and characters in a file. A 'word' is defined as a string of characters separated from the next by a space, tab or newline. It may therefore give slightly odd results with some program text files - but as the number of words in a program is usually irrelevant, that shouldn't matter.

Create a decent-sized file by running a long listing from the 'bin' into a file, then pass that to **wc**:

```
$ ls -l /bin >longbin
$ wc longbin
152   1361   8802 longbin
```

The first count is of lines, the next of words and the last of characters. You can have any one or two of these figure alone by setting the options **-l** for lines, **-w** for words and **-c** for characters:

```
$ wc -l longbin
152 longbin
$ wc -w longbin
1361 longbin
```

As elsewhere, the file specification can include wildcards. For a full breakdown of a directory, try:

```
$ wc -l *
6 add.c
61 bubble.pas
3 fax
12 filelist
164 Fincert.txt
134 sarah.let
3 fox
12 intest.pas
7 sum.c
1 temp
433 total
```

## **spell** - The Spelling Checker

We can't leave text processing without looking at **spell**. It is a quick and efficient spelling checker. The dictionary is extensive, but has the usual limitations over proper names and specialised terms - and even here, it compares well with the spell checkers included in professional word-processing packages. It is not difficult to your own supplementary list and link it into the checker. Unless you specify otherwise, the **spell** uses American spelling, but there is a British option for those who prefer 'realise' to 'realize', and 'colour' to 'color'.

A simple **spell**, followed by the filename, will produce a list of words that it cannot recognise.

```
$ spell memo
Heineman
arguement
seperately
thier
```

The list is arranged in ASCII order, which is very tidy, but not very helpful in terms of locating the errors within the file. Unfortunately there is no option which will give you the line numbers to assist in later editing. There is a simple solution to this problem. Redirect the output from **spell** into a file, then pass it to **fgrep** which can give you the context and line number.

```
$ spell memo >errors
$ fgrep -n -f errors memo          { -n for line numbers }
47:specialised word-processing application on thier Unix system
171:can take two types of numeric arguement. In theory, if you
205:There are three options, which can be used seperately or in
480:the well-known international publishers, Heinemann, whose
```

With a long file, the whole process may take a few moments - especially if your system is busy - and running a little slow. Improve your efficiency by combining the two commands into a single line, running the lot in the background and sending the final output to a file. The line is then:

```
$ (spell memo > errors ; fgrep -n -f errors memo >errlist ) &
```

You can then check the 'errlist' file later, and in the meantime can get on with other pressing jobs.

An alternative, or complementary, approach is to run the two commands together in a shell script. Using 'errors' as a standard name for the error list, your script should look like this:

```
spell $1 > errors          { $1 will collect the filename }
fgrep -n -f errors $1     { and pass it to fgrep }
```

## spell Options

There are two that are really useful:

**-b** selects **British** spelling

**+*filename*** makes **spell** cross-check with your own supplementary word list. This is a plain text file, containing one word on each line, sorted into simple ASCII order. To create your supplementary dictionary, collect **spell**'s output into an 'errors' file, each time you use it. Edit the file to remove any real errors, then **cat** the filtered list to the end of your permanent supplementary file - perhaps called 'wordlist'. This should then be sorted into order. The 'wordlist' can then be included in your command line next time you use **spell**.

```
$ cat errors >> wordlist     { append to supplementary file }
$ sort wordlist              { see Chapter 13 for sort }
....
$ spell +wordlist textfile > errors    { next time round }
```

## crypt - Encrypt or Decrypt a Text File

This is for those with sensitive data or personal secrets, or the just plain paranoid. Give **crypt** a password and a text file and it will produce an encrypted version. Give it the same password and the encrypted file to get your clear text back again. It offers a good level of security - the code could be broken by an expert armed with a Cray, or by anyone who knew your password, but not otherwise. The main gap in the security is at the moment

145

of encryption, for the password will be written in the command line.

**crypt** works on the standard input and output streams, so filenames must be given by redirection.

```
$ crypt enigma <myfile >mysecret
$ rm myfile
```

This has encrypted 'myfile' with 'enigma' as the password, and then removed it so that only the coded version remains.

```
$ crypt enigma <mysecret
```

This will decode the file and output it to the screen. To get a decoded file, redirect the output.

# Chapter 13

# Data File Processing

In Chapter 11, I touched on the idea of using Unix for data file processing, when introducing **grep**. You saw that, by finding lines that contained matching strings, **grep** could select records from a database. Let's look at the database concept and at some of the utilities that can manipulate data files in other ways.

## Databases

Even if you are not interested in databases, read on. The commands and techniques covered below can be applied to any organised files, and there are plenty of those in a Unix system.

Before we go any further, we should create some suitable files, so that we have something to work on. To be suitable, a file should have one record per line, with the fields separated by 'white space' - i.e. one or more space characters or tabs. The basic shape is:

|  | Field 1 | Field 2 | Field 3 | Field 4 | Field 5 |
|---|---|---|---|---|---|
| Record 1 |  |  |  |  |  |
| Record 2 |  |  |  |  |  |
| Record 3 |  |  |  |  |  |
| Record 4 |  |  |  |  |  |
| ..... |  |  |  |  |  |

In a business, such a file could hold stock data. Each record would hold the information for one type of goods, and the fields would be Reference

147

Number, Description, Supplier Reference, Quantity in Stock, Warehouse Location, and whatever. In a college, lecturers might use a database to store students' marks.

Within the Unix system there are many databases. The '/etc/passwd' file is a good example. Each line holds the essential data on a user - user name, ID number, group number, proper name, home directory, and login shell. Within every directory you will find another database - the file that holds the details of the files in the directory. You can't see it, but you can get at its contents by simply typing **ls**. A full listing has the classic database structure and will be ideal for demonstrating the use of data processing commands. Go to one of your smaller directories - half a dozen files or so will do nicely - and create a working copy of the listing with this:

```
$ ls -l > filelist          { collect the list in a file }
$ cat filelist              { and have a look at it }
total 12
-rwx————    1    mac  staff  4929  Nov 28 17:29 Fincert.txt
-rw-r—r—    1    mac  staff  400   Mar 18 10:57 Temp
-rw-r—r—    1    mac  staff  58    Nov 28 17:28 add.c
-rwx————    1    mac  staff  986   Nov 28 17:28 bubble.pas
-rw-r—r—    1    mac  staff  92    Oct 18 15:44 fax
-rw-r—r—    1    mac  staff  0     Nov 28 17:30 filelist
-rw-r—r—    1    mac  staff  689   Nov 15 12:20 sarah.let
-rw-r—r—    1    mac  staff  92    Oct 18 15:44 fox
-rw-r—r—    1    mac  staff  171   Nov 28 17:28 intest.pas
-rw-r—r—    1    mac  staff  62    Nov 28 17:28 sum.c
```

(Use **vi** to edit out that 'total' line. Its presence will only confuse matters.)

Each record has nine fields - permissions, links, owner, group, size, month, day, time and name. In the commands that allow you to specify fields, they are identified by number, counting from 0 on the left. Here, for instance, field 4 is the file size.

We will be wanting a second file later, and one where the separator is not the standard white space. This is the case with /etc/passwd, though there will probably be more than we need for example purposes. Use **grep** to slice out the records of one of the smaller groups on your system. The 'staff' group is the smallest on my system:

```
$ grep staff /etc/passwd >passlist
$ cat passlist
merlin:*:213:400:Nadia Felici,STAFF:/u/staff/merlin:/bin/csh
tony:*:201:400:Tony Millard,STAFF:/u/staff/tony:/bin/csh
mac:*:209:400:Mac Bride,STAFF:/u/staff/mac:/bin/csh
mike:*:207:400:Mike Turner,STAFF:/u/staff/mike:/bin/csh
tricia:*:211:400:Patricia Terndrup,STAFF:/u/staff/tricia:/bin/csh
dave:*:344:400:Dave Pittard:/u/staff/dave:/bin/csh
george:*:212:400:George Preston:/u/staff/george:/bin/csh
```

Your '/etc/passwd' file may not be structured in quite the same way. Some systems also hold the encoded passwords - as you might reasonably expect, given the file's name. The important point for our purposes is that the fields are separated by something other than white space - here the separator is the colon.

## sort - Sort a Data File into Order

By default, **sort** arranges the file into ASCII order, taking as its key the whole line, and sends its output to the screen. As it works on the ASCII sequence, all capitals come before lower case letters and numbers as treated as digits not values. And as it works on the whole line, the simple **sort** is not much use unless the key field happens to be the first. However, just to show how easy **sort** is to use - if the default settings apply - try it now with your 'filelist':

```
$ sort filelist
-rw-r—r—  1 mac    staff      0  Nov 28 17:30 filelist
-rw-r—r—  1 mac    staff    171 Nov 28 17:28 intest.pas
-rw-r—r—  1 mac    staff    400  Mar 18 10:57 Temp
-rw-r—r—  1 mac    staff     62  Nov 28 17:28 sum.c
-rw-r—r—  1 mac    staff    689  Nov 15 12:20 sarah.let
-rw-r—r—  1 mac    staff     58  Nov 28 17:28 add.c
-rw-r—r—  1 mac    staff     92  Oct 18 15:44 fax
-rw-r—r—  1 mac    staff     92  Oct 18 15:44 fox
-rwx———   1 mac    staff   4929  Nov 28 17:29 Fincert.txt
-rwx———   1 mac    staff    986  Nov 28 17:28 bubble.pas
```

Check your output and you should see a similar pattern. The order is determined firstly by the permissions - though these will be largely the same on all files - and then after that by file size. But look at the effect of sorting numbers by their ASCII codes, rather than values. "400" comes before "62"!

In most sorting operations, you will want the order to be determined by one or more specific fields. These may be in a group, scattered across the record or both, so it is not enough to give the field number. You must specify the first and last field number in each set. These are marked by a '+' for the first and '-' for the last (or more precisely, the next field after the sort keys.) So, **sort +2 -4 ...** would sort on fields 2 and 3 only.

If you give only the first, then the later fields are also used to determine order; likewise, by setting only the last field, the sort will use all the fields up to that point. So, for a single field sort, you need something like this:

**$ sort +5 -6 filelist**

```
-rw-r—r— 1 mac    staff     400  Mar 18 10:57 Temp
-rw-r—r— 1 mac    staff       0  Nov 28 17:30 filelist
-rwx———1 mac      staff    4929  Nov 28 17:29 Fincert.txt
-rwx———1 mac      staff     986  Nov 28 17:28 bubble.pas
-rw-r—r— 1 mac    staff     171  Nov 28 17:28 intest.pas
-rw-r—r— 1 mac    staff      62  Nov 28 17:28 sum.c
-rw-r—r— 1 mac    staff     689  Nov 15 12:20 sarah.let
-rw-r—r— 1 mac    staff      58  Nov 28 17:28 add.c
-rw-r—r— 1 mac    staff      92  Oct 18 15:44 fax
-rw-r—r— 1 mac    staff      92  Oct 18 15:44 fox
```

This sorts by month, field 5. To sort by month and then by name, you would have to specify fields 5 and 8, giving the command line:

**$ sort +5 -6 +8 filelist**

No 'last field' specification is needed for field 8, as there are no later fields.

If necessary, you can define the start and end more closely by specifying character positions within the fields. If you wanted to make the **minutes** a key in sorting the filelist, you would use:

## $ sort -n +7.3 -8 filelist

**sort** then skips over the first three characters of the time field to pick up the minutes at position 3.

## sort Options

**-f Folds** upper to lower case to produce a true alphabetical sort. Do you have a mixture of capitals and lower case in the names in your 'filelist'? If not, create a couple of new files (copying an existing one is the quickest way to do this) to give you a mixture, then run off a new version of the 'filelist'. Now try an alphabetic sort on the filenames - field 8:

### $ sort +8 filelist

| | | | | | | |
|---|---|---|---|---:|---|---|
| -rw-r—r— | 1 | mac | staff | 58 | Nov 28 17:28 | add.c |
| -rwx——— | 1 | mac | staff | 986 | Nov 28 17:28 | bubble.pas |
| -rw-r—r— | 1 | mac | staff | 92 | Oct 18 15:44 | fax |
| -rw-r—r— | 1 | mac | staff | 0 | Nov 28 17:30 | filelist |
| -rwx——— | 1 | mac | staff | 4929 | Nov 28 17:29 | Fincert.txt |
| -rw-r—r— | 1 | mac | staff | 92 | Oct 18 15:44 | fox |
| -rw-r—r— | 1 | mac | staff | 171 | Nov 28 17:28 | intest.pas |
| -rw-r—r— | 1 | mac | staff | 689 | Nov 15 12:20 | sarah.let |
| -rw-r—r— | 1 | mac | staff | 62 | Nov 28 17:28 | sum.c |
| -rw-r—r— | 1 | mac | staff | 400 | Mar 18 10:57 | Temp |

**-n** Treats **numbers** as values. With this option, we can do a proper sort by filesize. Set the option, then specify the field:

### $ sort -n +4 -5 filelist

| | | | | | | |
|---|---|---|---|---:|---|---|
| -rw-r—r— | 1 | mac | staff | 0 | Nov 28 17:30 | filelist |
| -rw-r—r— | 1 | mac | staff | 58 | Nov 28 17:28 | add.c |
| -rw-r—r— | 1 | mac | staff | 62 | Nov 28 17:28 | sum.c |
| -rw-r—r— | 1 | mac | staff | 92 | Oct 18 15:44 | fax |
| -rw-r—r— | 1 | mac | staff | 92 | Oct 18 15:44 | fox |
| -rw-r—r— | 1 | mac | staff | 171 | Nov 28 17:28 | intest.pas |
| -rw-r—r— | 1 | mac | staff | 400 | Mar 18 10:57 | Temp |
| -rw-r—r— | 1 | mac | staff | 689 | Nov 15 12:20 | sarah.let |
| -rwx———1 | | mac | staff | 986 | Nov 28 17:28 | bubble.pas |
| -rwx———1 | | mac | staff | 4929 | Nov 28 17:29 | Fincert.txt |

**-M** (Notice the capitals) sorts by **Month.** It first forces the characters in the field to capitals, then sorts in order "JAN" to "DEC". It works equally well with abbreviations and full month names. Combine this with a numeric sort on the day field to put 'filelist' into date order:

```
$ sort -M +5 -6 -n +6 -7 filelist
-rw-r—r—  1 mac    staff     400   Mar 18 10:57 Temp
-rw-r—r—  1 mac    staff      92   Oct 18 15:44 fox
-rw-r—r—  1 mac    staff      92   Oct 18 15:44 fax
-rw-r—r—  1 mac    staff     689   Nov 15 12:20 sarah.let
-rw-r—r—  1 mac    staff       0   Nov 28 17:30 filelist
-rw-r—r—  1 mac    staff      58   Nov 28 17:28 add.c
-rw-r—r—  1 mac    staff      62   Nov 28 17:28 sum.c
-rw-r—r—  1 mac    staff     171   Nov 28 17:28 intest.pas
-rwx———   1 mac    staff     986   Nov 28 17:28 bubble.pas
-rwx———   1 mac    staff    4929   Nov 28 17:29 Fincert.txt
```

**-o** *filename* Sends **Output** to the named file - though here as elsewhere, redirection can be used to create files. If there is an existing file of the given name, it will be overwritten. This line will create a new file, sorted in alphabetical order of the filenames - field 9.

```
$ sort -o sortfile -f +9 filelist
```

**-t***char* Sets *char* as the **separator**, instead of the usual white space. For this example, we will use 'passlist', generated from the '/etc/passwd' file, where the separator is a colon and spaces have no special significance. Write the new separator immediately after the '-t'.

```
$ sort -t: -n +2 -3 passlist
tony:*:201:400:Tony Millard,STAFF:/u/staff/tony:/bin/csh
mike:*:207:400:Mike Turner,STAFF:/u/staff/mike:/bin/csh
mac:*:209:400:Mac Bride,STAFF:/u/staff/mac:/bin/csh
tricia:*:211:400:Patricia Terndrup,STAFF:/u/staff/tricia:/bin/csh
george:*:212:400:George Preston:/u/staff/george:/bin/csh
merlin:*:213:400:Nadia Felici,STAFF:/u/staff/merlin:/bin/csh
dave:*:344:400:Dave Pittard:/u/staff/dave:/bin/csh
```

**-r Reverses** the sort order. It can be used by itself or in combination with '-f' or '-n'. Try it, combined it with '-n' to sort 'filelist' into order of size, with the largest first:

**$ sort -r -n +5 -6 -o filesize filelist**

N.B. **The order of options** is largely irrelevant. All that really matters is that command starts with **sort** and ends with the input filename. These lines would all work just as well:

**$ sort -n +5 -6 -r -o filesize filelist**
**$ sort -o filesize -r -n +5 -6 filelist**
**$ sort -r -o filesize -n +5 -6 filelist**

## cut - Cut Vertically through a File

This command is designed to cut fields out of a database, but will also slice a column of characters - of any width - out of a text file. It has two distinct modes of operation, working either by characters or by fields.

**cut** is basically straightforward, though a couple of minor alterations in its design would have made it easier to use. The first point to note is that **cut**, unlike **sort**, does not recognise 'white space' (any string of spaces or a tab) as a field separator. The default separator for **cut** is the tab. You can specify an alternative character as the separator - but only a single character. As a result, if you have two fields separated by a string of spaces there's no way you can get it to skip over those spaces. This doesn't actually stop you from slicing space-separated files, but you have to tackle them differently.

The second difference from **sort**, is that in **cut**, the fields are numbered from 1, not 0. It is a trivial difference, but if they had been the same in these respects, the techniques used with **sort** could have been carried over to **cut**, and vice versa - and you would make fewer errors with them both.

**cut** options are not particularly complex, but they are interdependent and we will tackle them as we come to them. Note that there is no option for output to file. The results will normally appear on the screen or be piped on to another command. If you do want to store the output, use the > redirect to send it to a file.

## -f Cutting by Fields

If the fields are tab-separated, then the command takes the form:

**cut -f *field-list file***

The *field-list* can contain single field numbers - counting from 1, or ranges. The fields in the list are separated by commas. For example, to cut field 3 and all those between 6 and 10 from a tab-separated file called 'mydata':

**$ cut -f 3,6-7 mydata**

If the file uses an *alternative separator* character, define this with the **-d** option. It may only be a single character - there is no way to get **cut** to recognise variable length spaces. Test the option with your 'passlist' file, where the separator is the colon:

**$ cut -d: -f5,1,7 ../passlist**
merlin:Nadia Felici,STAFF:/bin/csh
tony:Tony Millard,STAFF:/bin/csh
mac:Mac Bride,STAFF:/bin/csh
mike:Mike Turner,STAFF:/bin/csh
tricia:Patricia Terndrup,STAFF:/bin/csh
dave:Dave Pittard:/bin/csh
george:George Preston:/bin/csh

The order in which fields are listed is unimportant. Whatever order you use, the output will always be in field order. You can see that here, where the input list was 5, 1, 7 but the output is in the order 1, 5, 7.

If a line has no separators characters in it, it is normally output intact. This can be useful as it means that table headings and annotation lines are carried across from the original file. These would not occur in most datafiles, but are found in files that are themselves reports from a database. If you want to suppress these, use the **-s** option. e.g.

**$ cut -s -f3-5,7,9 mydata.rpt**

This cuts fields 3 to 5 and field 7 from the report, and also removes any header lines.

## -c Cutting by Position

This option is selected by **-c**, and is the way to deal with files that are separated by spaces, as long as the spacing is such that the data for each field starts and ends in an identifiable column. This is the case with our 'filelist' example. Identifying the columns can be a bit of a bother. The best bet may well be to load it into **vi** or a word-processor. Most have a status line that displays the row and column position of the cursor, so by moving the cursor along a line, you can read off the appropriate column numbers. At worst, you can move the cursor one character at a time and count!

```
0         1         2         3         4         5         6
1234567890123456789012345678901234567890123456789012345678901 2345
-rw-r—r— 1 mac   staff            0 Nov 28 17:30  filelist
-rw-r—r— 1 mac   staff          171 Oct 29 14:32  intest.pas
-rw-r—r— 1 mac   staff          400 Mar 18 10:57  Temp
-rw-r—r— 1 mac   staff           62 Nov 10 13:49  sum.c
-rw-r—r— 1 mac   staff          689 Nov 15 12:20  sarah.let
-rw-r—r— 1 mac   staff           58 Nov 20 14:05  add.c
-rw-r—r— 1 mac   staff           92 Oct 18 15:44  fax
-rw-r—r— 1 mac   staff           92 Oct 18 15:44  fox
-rwx——— 1 mac    staff         4929 Nov 28 17:29  Fincert.txt
-rwx——— 1 mac    staff          986 Oct 24 11:14  bubble.pas
```

Suppose we wanted to cut the filesize and names out of 'filelist'. We can work out that the filesizes all fit between columns 35 and 40, and that the names start at column 54 and run to 65. (Yours may well be different - position largely depends upon the tab settings of your terminal.)

```
$ cut -c35-40,54-65 filelist
4929 Fincert.txt
400 Temp
58 add.c
986 bubble.pas
92 fax
0 filelist
92 fox
171 intest.pas
689 sarah.let
62 sum.c
```

That space between the sizes and names is there because it was included in the name-cut. If its position had been given as 55-65, i.e. starting at the first letter of the name, there would have been no space.

As with the field-based option, this cut outputs its sets of characters in the same order as they were in the original file, no matter how you list them in the command line. If you want to cut columns and rearrange their order, the answer is to cut each one into a separate file, them splice them back together with **paste**. **cut** them now, and you will be ready for **paste** when we get to it in a moment. Redirect the filesizes to a file called 'sizes', the dates and times to 'dates', and the names to one called 'names'.

```
$ cut -c35-40 filelist > sizes
$ cut -c42-53 filelist > dates
$ cut -c54-65 filelist > names
```

**cut** works well in pipes, as long as you know the field structure of the output of the previous command. For example, you could find the login IDs and full names of all the Pauls on your system by this combination of **grep** and **cut**.

```
$ grep -i paul /etc/passwd | cut -d: -f 1,5
pixi:Paul McGovern,NDCS2B
cleric:Paul Burnett,NDCS2B
hawk:Paul Godden,NDCS1A
pelican:Paul Taylor,NDCS1B
earth:Paul Hannan,NCCS1A
asteroid:Paul McMullen,NCCS1IT
silkcut:Paul Smith,NDITA1
```

**paste** - Merge Files by Column

At the simplest, this takes a number of files, each consisting of a column of text, and arranges them side by side. For example, to produce a list of filenames followed by their sizes, we would use:

**$ paste names sizes**

| | |
|---|---|
| Fincert.txt | 4929 |
| Temp | 400 |
| add.c | 58 |
| bubble.pas | 986 |
| fax | 92 |
| filelist | 0 |
| fox | 92 |
| intest.pas | 171 |
| sarah.let | 689 |
| sum.c | 62 |

The result may well not be as neat as this! The pasted columns here are separated by tabs, the default separator. As a result, if an item in the first column overruns a tab position, the corresponding item in the second column will be pushed to the next tab position. If you want to produce a file for print-out, then a little work with **vi** or a word-processor may be necessary.

## paste Options

**-d** *list* **Defines** an alternative set of separators With this option the command takes the form:

**paste -d** *list* **file1 file2 file...**

The *list* is a set of one or more characters to be used - one at a time - as separators. When **paste** reaches the end of the list, it cycles back to the start and runs through them again. The end of each line is always terminated by a newline, no matter what characters you use in the list. Any characters can be used, but note the special escape combinations:

| | |
|---|---|
| \\**t** | tab space |
| \\**n** | newline |
| \\ | backslash |
| \\**0** | null string - i.e. no separator |

The characters here are those recognised by the C language. Note the double slashes! The backslash has a special meaning to the shell (it 'escapes' the following character), so to get it past the shell and through to the **paste** command, it must itself be escaped. The first backslash is then stripped off by the shell, and the second one gives 't', 'n' and '0' their special meanings in **paste**. To paste together our sample files in the order date, name and size, with a colon after the date and a tab after the name, we would need the line:

```
$ paste -d|\\t dates names sizes
Nov 27 17:29: Fincert.txt 4929
Mar 18 10:57: Temp       400
Nov 10 14:05: add.c      58
Oct 24 11:14: bubble.pas 986
Mar 18 10:57: fax        92
Nov 28 17:28: filelist   0
Nov 28 17:28: fox        92
Oct 29 14:32: intest.pas 171
Nov 15 12:20: sarah.let  689
Nov 10 13:49: sum.c      62
```

**-s** Pastes **successive** lines across the screen. With this option you can break one long list down into a set of columns, to make it fit more compactly on screen or paper. Use 'binlist' - the file created by redirecting the **ls** listing from the 'bin' - or any other suitable file. **paste** it across the screen with:

```
$ paste -s binlist
STTY       acctcom adb     ar      as      asm      auths
basenamebfs        cat     cc      chgrp   chkshlib chmod
chown      chroot  clear   cmp     conv    convert  copy
cp         cpio    cprs    csh     date    dd       df
diff       dirname dis     dos     dparam  dtype    du
dump       echo    ed      env     expr    false    login
lorder     lr      ls      lx      mail    make     masm
mc68k      mesg    mkdir   mkshlib mt      mv       ncheck
newgrp     nice    nm      nohup   od      passwd   pdp11
pr         printenv ps     pstat   pwd     ranlib   rcc
red        rm      rmdir   rsh     sddate  sed      setkey
setpgrp    whodo   write   wtty    x286emulxbackupxdump
xdumpdir   xrestor xrestore yes
```

Unlike the simple **paste**, this -s version does not put newlines at the end of each line across. This doesn't matter on screen, but if you pasting to a file that will be printed, it can play havoc with the layout on paper. In this situation, decide how many columns you would like then supply a list of tabs and newlines with the -d option. For example, for a four column layout of the \bin list, you would use:

```
$ paste -s -d\\t\\t\\t\\n binlist
STTY     [          acctcom adb
ar       as         asm     auths
....
who      whodo      write   wtty
x286emul xbackup    xdump   xdumpdir
xrestor  xrestore   yes
```

## Multiple Files and Multiple Columns

If you use **-s** with more than one file, it pastes the first file into columns, then starts the second on a new line below it. This is probably not as you would like it, as it destroys any links between the items in the files. If you did want to paste two files and arrange them in, say, three pairs of columns across the page, then it would take two operations. These can be run on two separate lines - the first to create an intermediate two-column file; the second to split this into three columns. The separator list will require two tabs and a newline.

```
$ paste names sizes > temp
$ paste -s -d\\t\\t\\n temp
add.c    58    bubble.pas    986  fax          92
filelist 0     Fincert.txt   4929 fox          92
intest.pas     171  sarah.let     689  sum.c    62
Temp     400
```

(As usual, tab does not necessarily produce neat columns.)

Alternatively, the two commands can be piped together:

**$ paste names sizes | paste -s -d\\t\\t\\n -**

Note that dash at the end of the line. If you are piping into **paste**, the dash replaces the input filename.

Which ever way you do it, the problem of uneven spacing means that the final result is not always as organised as you might like.

## join - Combine Two Data Files

This command is for use with relational databases - i.e. sets of files that are linked by a common key field. In a commercial environment, a typical database would be one to manage the stock. It would consist of two files. The first would hold the details for each stock line. e.g.

StockRef    Description    SupplierRef    QuantityInStock    ...

The second would hold the supplier information:

SupplierRef    Name    Address1    Address2    ...

Splitting the data into two files is far more efficient that holding it all in one. If there was only a single stock file, it would have to hold the supplier's details for each stock line - and if a firm supplied a dozen different items, its name and address would appear a dozen times. Apart from increasing the quantity of data stored, such duplication makes updating a real headache. If a supplier moved premises, someone would have to track down and alter every copy of the details. With the two file approach, a single correction is all that is needed.

The 'SupplierRef' field is common to both, and makes the link between the two files. With this as a key, you can produce a report that draws selected data from both files. When reordering goods, you would pull the descriptions, references, order quantities and prices from the first file, and the suppliers' names and addresses from the second.

To see how **join** works, you will need some suitable files. If there are none around on your system that you can play with, then use **cut** and **paste** to make some of your own. Each file should have at least two fields, one of which will be common to all, and they must be sorted into order by their key field.

160

Some files made up of cuttings from your 'filelist' will do nicely. You should already have 'names', sizes' and 'dates' extracts. Cut out two more files containing the permissions and the links - or any other fields - variety is all that is needed.

```
$ cut -c-10 filelist > perms
$ cut -c11-12 filelist > links
```

**paste** them together to make three new files. One will have names, sizes and links; the second names and dates; the third links, sizes, names and permissions. The overlap of contents is intentional, as is the positioning of the 'names' field.

```
$ paste names sizes links > temp1        { names in field 1 }
$ paste names dates > temp2              { names in field 1 }
$ paste sizes names perms > temp3        { names in field 2 }
```

Now sort them into order by key field - remembering that in **sort** the fields are numbered from 0:

```
$ sort +0 -1 -o file1 temp1
$ sort +0 -1 -o file2 temp2
$ sort +1 -2 -o file3 temp3
```

If you don't tell it otherwise, **join** assumes that the key field is the first in each file, and that you want to include all the fields in the output.

```
$ join file1 file2
Fincert.txt 4929 1 Nov 28 17:29
Temp 400 1 Mar 18 1992
add.c 58 1 Nov 10 14:05
bubble.pas 986 1 Oct 24 11:14
fax 92 1 Oct 18 15:44
filelist 0 1 Nov 28 17:30
fox 92 1 Oct 18 15:44
intest.pas 171 1 Oct 29 14:32
sarah.let 689 1 Nov 15 12:20
sum.c 62 1 Nov 10 14:05
```

The irregular spacing does nothing for clarity, but you should be able to see that the fields are output in the order name, size, links and date. That is, the key field followed by the remaining fields of the first file then those of the second.

## join Options

**-j** Sets a **new key field**. Use this option where the key field is not the first in a line. The key is identified by the file and field number, counting the first as 1 in both cases.

For example, to join 'file1' and 'file3', the name field must be identified in the latter file. If 'file3' is listed second, then the file number is 2 and the name is the second field, the field number is also 2. That gives us:

```
$ join -j2 2 file1 file3
Fincert.txt 4929 1 4929 -rwx————
Temp 400 1 400 -rw-r—r—
add.c 58 1 58 -rw-r—r—
bubble.pas 986 1 986 -rwx————
fax 92 1 92 -rw————-
filelist 0 1 0 -rw-r—r—
fox 92 1 92 -rw————-
intest.pas 171 1 171 -rw-r—r—
sarah.let 689 1 689 -rw-r—r—
sum.c 62 1 62 -rw-r—r—
```

Of course, if we had given the files in the order 'file3 file1', the option would have read '**-j1 2**'. And note the punctuation in the **-j** option. There isn't any! The file and field numbers are simply separated by a space. If necessary, give the key field numbers for both files, including the **-j** with each.

If, for instance, the key field appeared in third place in the first file and sixth in the second, the command line would start:

```
$ join -j1 3 -j2 6
```

**-o** *list* Defines the **output** fields. You may have noticed that the sizes are given twice in that last output, as they were present in both input files. If you have duplication, or any other unwanted fields, you can refine the output by listing the fields which are to appear.

As with **-j**, the fields are identified by file and field number, but this time there is punctuation! The numbers are separated by a dot. The order in which the fields are listed determined the order that they appear in the output.

For example, here is what we need to get fields from 'file1' and 'file3' in the order:

name (1.1 or 2.1), permissions (2.3), size (1.2) and links (1.3)

```
$join -j2 2 -o 1.1 2.3 1.2 1.3 file1 file3
Fincert.txt -rwx——— 4929 1
Temp -rw-r—r— 400 1
add.c -rw-r—r— 58 1
bubble.pas -rwx——— 986 1
fax -rw——— 92 1
filelist -rw-r—r— 0 1
fox -rw——— 92 1
intest.pas -rw-r—r— 171 1
sarah.let -rw-r—r— 689 1
sum.c -rw-r—r— 62 1
```

**-t***char* Defines the *character* as the alternative separator. The simple **join** assumes that the separators between fields in the input file will be spaces (any number of them), tab or newline, and it uses a single space as the separator in the output. Use this option to set an alternative character as the separator - noting that it will apply to both the input and output.

### $ join -t: passlist grouplist

This would combine files where the separator was a colon.

## join in Pipes

**join** can only ever work on two files, though the first file can be replaced by input from the keyboard or a piped command. Within a pipe, **join** takes the form:

> *... earlier command(s)* | join [options] - *file*

Note the dash to indicate input from the earlier command. It may replace either the first or second file.

# Chapter 14

# File Maintenance

One of the nice things about a multi-user system is that all the routine backing up of files is usually done for you by the system administrator. Keeping files safe is not the chore that is can be on a stand-alone PC - but keeping files tidy and organised is probably more of a chore. I suspect the problem is that you have apparently unlimited disk space. It's not unlimited, of course, and the system administrator will no doubt be breathing down your neck if spread yourself too freely. But there are no regular reminders of how little space is left. On a PC, every time you do a DIR to find a file, there's a note of the free space at the end of the list. **ls** doesn't do this, and even **du** only tells you how much you have used, not how much remains. As a result, most of us tend to leave files on the system long after they have ceased to be of use. And as a result of that, our directories tend to clog up. The main focus of this chapter is sorting out what to do with those files that are no longer in regular use.

## Directory Management

Regular and brutal wielding of the **rm** axe is probably the best way to save space and keep directories tidy, but that is too painful for those of us who are anal-retentives, and too final for those trying to build a body of files for assessment, demonstration or development purposes. For these, other approaches must be found. Let's remind ourselves that we are trying to do two things - save space and keep directories tidy.

Good directory management is mainly a matter of structure and working habits, rather than of using any special commands. You should by now have created separate directories for each area of your work. If they have been filled beyond a convenient size - i.e. so that a full listing more than fills the screen - now is the time to trim and to sub-divide. First, remove those that really are of no further use, and any compiled programs that are not immediately wanted, though retaining the source code so that they can be recompiled later. Compiled programs tend to be large - on the SCO Unix system that I work with, a typical 20k Cobol text file compiles into a 300+k program. If a straight **rm** is too final for you, make deletion a two-stage process. Set up a new directory called 'junk' (or something similar). Then instead of removing a file, move it to this directory, from which it can be reclaimed if wanted. At the end of every week or so, check your 'junk', and clear out those files that are clearly surplus. If you work in a C shell, you can create an alias to manage the move/remove efficiently.

### % alias junkit 'rm $1 ~/junk'

For long-term storage, create a new sub-directory, perhaps called 'old', and move into it those that are no longer in regular use but may be wanted later. Each directory should have its own 'old', so that files can be moved easily in and out of cold storage.

If there are still too many active files in the same place, look for ways that you could logically sub-divide them. It's best to make the new directory at the same level as the split one, rather than a sub-directory of it.

For example, a computer science student has a directory structure as shown in Figure 14.1. The 'programs' directory has grown to the point where something must be done. Most of the programs are in Pascal, but recently she has started working in C. Looking ahead, she can see that she will be producing a lot more Pascal files, and that they will fall into two main groups - mathematical and file-handling. By and large, once a program is finished, it is not normally needed again, but can be useful for reference. Such files should be stashed away in a sub-directory.

**Figure 14.1**

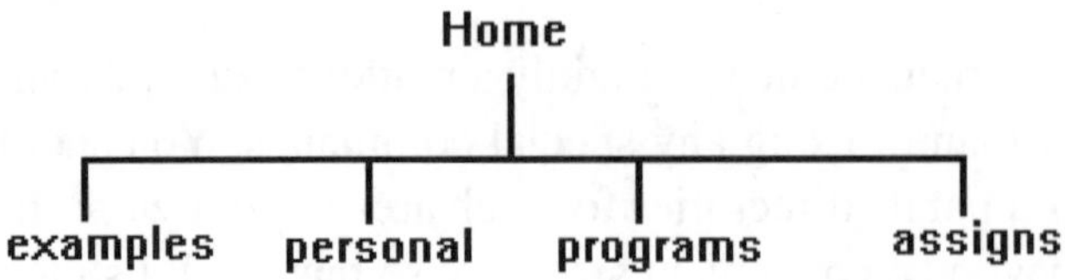

166

Figures 14.2 shows a possible reorganisations of the structure. In 14.2, 'programs' has disappeared and been replaced by 'filepas', 'mathpas', 'otherpas' and 'C'. Each of these has a single sub-directory called 'old', and contains the old files of its parent directory. No file is more than two levels down, so that, working from the home directory, the longest pathname that ever has to be used is 'otherpas/old'.

**Figure 14.2**

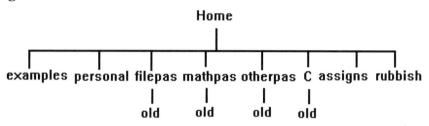

In Figure 14.3 we see how the directory structure would be if our student took the sub-sub-sub- approach. 'programs' has been divided into 'Pascal' and 'C'. 'Pascal' is then divided into 'maths', 'files' and 'others'. There will now by paths such as 'programs/Pascal/other/old'. Try typing that correctly in a hurry, and you will see why it's best to have as few levels as possible.

**Figure 14.3**

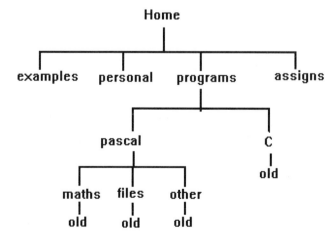

## Saving Space

### pack - Compress Files

If a file is being placed into cold storage, it may as well take as little disk space as possible. The **pack** command will compress a file, removing the original and replacing it by one marked with a **.z** extension. How much compression is achieved depends upon the type of file. Typically, **pack** will only manage a 15% saving on a compiled file, but 50% or more with text files.

It is generally not worth trying to pack files of less than 2k, as the extra code needed to interpret the compression takes more space than that saved by packing. **pack** checks on possible saving, and will abandon the effort if it is not worth while. There are other situations where **pack** will not work - principally inability to access the target file, but long filenames are also a problem.

At the simplest, the command is simply followed by the name:

> **$ pack bigprog.pas**
> pack: bigprog.pas: 43.8% Compression

The packed file will be called 'bigprog.pas.z' and will replace the original 'bigprog.pas'.

### pack options.

**-f forces** the packing, even where there is no saving. This is mainly of value where you want to use a wildcard expression on a set of files, prior to putting them into cold storage.

> **$ pack -f *.txt**
> **$ mv *.z old**

With this sequence, all text files have been compressed then moved into the 'old' directory. Even with **-f** selected, **pack** will still fail on long filenames. Unix only recognises the first 14 characters of a filename, and

168

as the **.z** extension must be recognisable, for later unpacking, the original name cannot be more than 12 characters.

```
$ pack -f st*
pack: stars: 19.4% Compression          { compiled }
pack: stars.pas: 24.0% Compression      { short text }
pack: stocktest.pas: file name too long { 13 characters }
pack: string.pas: 27.5% Compression
pack: stringtest.pas: file name too long
pack: strnum.pas: 29.3% Compression
pack: student.cbl: 51.2% Compression    { long text, packs well }
```

The second option is selected by a plain **dash**, with no identifying initial. (Don't you just wish that Unix commands all worked to the same pattern!) This is for diagnostic purposes, and tells you just what **pack** has done to your file.

```
$ pack - network.txt
pack: network.txt: 49.4% Compression
from 4323 to 2185 bytes
Huffman tree has 13 levels below root
74 distinct bytes in input
dictionary overhead  = 94 bytes
effective  entropy    = 4.04 bits/byte
asymptotic entropy  = 3.87 bits/byte
```

So now you know. Try this with a small file and you will see that the saving in bytes can well be less than the dictionary overhead.

Note that, unlike the DOS compression utilities in common use, **pack** works on a single file basis. You cannot **pack** a set of files into one compressed file. Merging them into a single file after compression would be ill-advised as there is no simple means to separate them again.

If you want to keep the compressed files in one place, create a special directory and stick them in there, or read on and find out about **cpio**.

## unpack - Restore Packed Files

**unpack** restores your original file. When using it, you can omit the **.z** extension, as **unpack** will check for that anyway.

### $ unpack network.txt

This will search for a file called 'network.txt.z', uncompress it into 'network.txt' and remove the compressed copy.

## pcat - Packed File Concatenation

**pcat** is the **cat** equivalent for packed files. Use it to view, without unpacking, or redirect the output to save an unpacked copy without removing the compressed file.

```
$ pcat thing.pas          {view the file}
$ pcat funcs.c.z >funcs.c  {unpack but retain the packed file}
```

## cpio - Copy In from and Out to Devices

This is primarily for copying to and from archive (backup) files on external storage devices - tapes and floppy disks - and device management is the province of the system administrator, and beyond the scope of this book. However, **cpio** has features which make it of interest to ordinary users.

The first is that, used in conjunction with **find**, **cpio** will copy selected files from locations throughout a directory structure. If you were copying for backup purposes, the ones you would be finding would be those that had been changed since the last time you did a backup. Their paths are recorded, by **cpio**, as they are copied. The other major feature is that when you copy a set of files with **cpio**, the output is in the form of a single file. Copied back in again, the archive file separates into its original components. Individual files, or wildcard selections, can be copied back as required, and restored files will drop back into their original directories.

What this means for 'cold storage' purposes, is that, instead of a collection of separate files, you can turn a set of inactive files into one single file, and - this is important - that **cpio** file can be packed, saving substantial amounts of space.

**cpio** is one of the more complex commands, with a large set of options. Fortunately, you can ignore most of them when you are copying to and from a file. To test it, go into your 'examples' directory, and check that this contains at least one sub-directory with some files in it. As the testing process is potentially destructive, these files should be dispensable. (All being well you will recover the files that you will remove while testing - that is the object of the exercise - but mistakes do happen.) If necessary, create a new sub-directory and copy a few files into it. You might also like to create a new directory called 'archives', or something similar, up at the top level, parallel to 'examples'.

## cpio Options

**-o** selects **outward** copying. The command itself is a bare **cpio -o**, for the source files and target archive are not given as part of the command. The list of files to be copied is piped in, usually from a **find** but sometimes from an **ls** command, and the output is redirected to the archive file. For example:

**$ find . -print | cpio -o > backup.cpio**

As the **find** in this example has no limiting pattern, it locates all the files in the current, and subordinate, directories. The **-print** option generates a list of filenames. These are fed into **cpio**, which archives them into a file called 'backup.cpio'. Try it in your 'examples' directory, then run an **ls** to make sure that it is there.

**$ find . -ctime 0 -print | cpio -o > ../archives/dec15.bak**

This time, **find** is being used selectively, and the output has been redirected to a file in the 'archives' directory.

171

**-i** selects **Inward** copying from an archive file. For obvious reasons, either this or **-o** must be given as one of the options.

The assumption here is that you will want to select certain files for recovery from the archive. These are specified by a wildcard expression, using the standard shell metacharacters, **\* ? [ ]**. As with outward copying, the archive file is accessed by redirection.

Try this to test the inwards copying. (You did create 'backup.cpio' earlier, didn't you? You need it now.) There should be several files starting with 'f' in the 'examples' directory. Remove one or two - but not all of them, then gove the command:

   **$ cpio -i f\* < backup.cpio**

This will copy in from the archive, those files starting with 'f' which are not there already. **cpio** will not normally overwrite existing files of the same name.

**-u** causes the inward copying to be **unconditional.** With this option set, archive files will overwrite existing ones of the same name. Try it. Edit one of your 'f...' files, and give this command:

   **$ cpio -iu f\* <backup.cpio**

Now examine relevant file. You should find that you are back to your previous version.

**-v** This **verbose** option can be used on both Inward and Outward copying. It displays the names of files as they are accessed. To pass all the files in the current directory across to an archive, and watch them as they go, try this:

   **$ ls | cpio -ov >newback.cpio**

**-t** creates a **Table of Contents** to show you what is in an archive. It must be used with the -i option, though it does not do any actual copying.

**$ cpio -it < backup.cpio**

```
.
filelist
fox
fax
...
...
backup/names
backup/binlist
bak
memo
errors
mydic
36 blocks
```

**-d** Creates **Directories** as needed. Use this to recreate a directory structure - either in a different part of the system, or because the original structure has been destroyed. As **cpio** reads files from the archives, it gets the pathname that was saved with them. Normally it will use this to drop the files into their rightful places - but only if the directories exist. With this option set, it will create suitable directories if necessary. A certain amount of caution is therefore needed when using this. Do make sure that you are in the right point in your directory structure before giving the command.

To test it out, clear the 'dispensable' sub-directory of the files that you put there for testing, then remove the directory itself. now try:

**$ cpio -id <backup.cpio**

Run an **ls** and you should find that the directory is back.

Finally, back to space-saving. Once you have archived your files, you can compress them, to give you a neat, compact 'cold-store'.

**$ find . -ctime 0 -print | cpio -o >dec15.arc**
**$ pack dec15.arc**

# Chapter 15

# Miscellaneous Utilities

This is a bit of a rag-bag of a chapter, bringing together a number of commands and programs that don't really have anything in common except that they don't fit comfortably into other chapters. Perhaps I am being a little unfair to them. Most are the sort of things that are often found as pop-up programs in modern DOS systems. I could have grouped them under the heading 'Productivity Software', except that I regard this as a term invented by someone's marketing department to cover a rag-bag of programs that didn't really have anything in common.

**banner** - Sign Maker

Use this to create a cheery login or logout screen, to make cover pages for reports or send hard-to-ignore mail to other users. **banner** takes text strings and echoes them back to the screen in characters 8 rows high. The output can, of course, be >redirected to a file for printing or for mailing to others. The text can be as long as you like with these limitations: each string - either a single word or a set enclosed in quotes - may not have more than 10 characters; as each string is started on a new row, and the rows are well spaced out, you can only fit two full rows on screen, or five or six on a page.

```
$ banner 'Think BIG'
XXXXX X       X         X       XXXX   XXX   XXXX
  X   X                 X       X  X   X     X
  X   XXXX  XX   XXXX  X  X     X  X   X     X
  X   X  X   X   X  X  X  X X    XXXX   X     X  XX
  X   X  X   X   X  X  XXX       X  X   X     X   X
  X   X  X   X   X  X  X  X      X  X   X     X   X
  X   X  X  XXX  X  X  X   X     XXXX   XXX   XXXX
```

175

## bc - Programmable Calculator

This is both an interactive calculator and a programming language. To use it interactively, start it up with a simple **bc** then type in your calculations. An expression given by itself will be evaluated and the answer displayed immediately; but the result of the expression may be assigned to a variable, and the result will be stored for use in later calculations.

**bc** can handle the usual range of arithmetic operators and expressions written in C-style syntax. Variables do not need declaring before they are used, and any suitable names can be used, as long as they start with lower case letters. (Upper case letters are reserved for Hexadecimal characters.) Try this sequence - or some calculations of your own.

```
$ bc          { start up in interactive mode }
2 + 3         { spaces are optional }
5             { the answer is displayed }
n=2^4         { the result (16) is stored in the new variable n }
n+=10         { C-style += symbol, equivalent to n=n+10 }
n             { variable name given by itself ... }
26            { ... produces the answer }
[Ctrl]-[D]        { to exit }
```

As a programming language, **bc** is effectively a sub-set of C, with the same key words and structures. The calculation sequence is written into a file, then passed to **bc** on start-up in the form 'bc filename'.

If you are already familiar with C, then **bc** is easily mastered - though there's little point in making the effort, as you may as well stick to C if you want to progam your calculations.

## cal - Calendar Maker

This will give you a calendar for any month or year, from the year dot to way past the point where you will care what the date is. Specify the month alone for a month in the current year, or add the year - in 4-digit format - if necessary.

```
$ cal dec 1993
    December
Su Mo TuWe Th  Fr Sa
             1   2  3  4
 5  6  7  8  9 10 11
12 13 14 15 16 17 18
19 20 21 22 23 24 25
26 27 28 29 30 31
```

**cal** followed by a year number only, will produce a calendar for the whole year, but redirect the output to a file as it won't fit on screen.

```
$ cal 1993 >cal93
```

Now you can print your own calendar and save the expense of buying one.

## calendar - Reminder Service

For this to work, you should have a file in your HOME directory called 'calendar', containing a list of dates and events for which you need reminders. The file layout should follow the pattern given here, with each line having 'Month Day Message'. The lines do not have to be in date order, and months can be given as full names, abbreviations or by number values - but it must always be month before day.

```
Dec 31 Final Deadline
Jan 4 Ms to Typesetter
Jan 18 Page proofs back?
Jan 25 Index & corrected proofs
Feb 12 CRC to printers
Mar 4 Books due in warehouse
```

Just type **calendar** to check on the messages for today and tomorrow - with Friday's tomorrow extending to Monday.

Your system administrator may already be running **calendar** as a service to users, doing a daily check on your file and sending you reminders by mail. If it is not there, write the command into your '.login' file, for your own start-of-day reminder service.

## **dc** - The Desk Calculator

**dc** is an interactive calculator that works in reverse Polish notation. If you have not previously come across this before, it is worth a look just to see how it works. If you are already familiar with it, then here is a calculator that you can use.

The essence of reverse Polish, is that you write the numbers first and the operators afterwards. As numbers are received, they are stored on the *stack*. This is a temporary memory store that runs on the Last In, First Out principle. When an operator is received, **dc** takes the last two numbers off the stack, performs the operation on them and puts the answer back on the stack. The value at the top of the stack can be viewed by the command **p** (print), and removed by **c** (clear). See how it works by trying this sequence:

```
$ dc              { run the program }
2 3 +             { 2 & 3 on the stack, + takes them off and adds }
p                 { print the top value }
5
4                 { store 4 - stack now holds 5 & 4 }
*                 { take off 4 & 5 and multiply }
p
20
c                 { clear the stack }
3 4 5 + *         { see Note 1 }
p
27
5 4 3 + 2 - * p       { see Note 2 }
q  { quit }
```

Note 1: A calculation string can have any number of terms. Here, **dc** will first store 3, 4 and 5. Meeting '+' it will then take off 4 and 5 - the top two - and add them, putting the result back on the stack. It then reaches '*' and multiplies 9 and 3 to get the answer.

Note 2: You may need to intermingle operators and numbers to get the right sequence of calculations. Here is what happens as **dc** works through this string.

| Input | Action | Stack |
|-------|--------|-------|
| 5 | stack it | 5 |
| 4 | stack it | 4 5 |
| 3 | stack it | 3 4 5 |
| + | add and stack the result | 7 5 |
| 2 | stack it | 2 7 5 |
| - | subtract and stack the result | 5 5 |
| * | multiply and stack the result | 2 5 |
| p | print the result | 2 5 |

Real enthusiasts will be pleased to know that **dc** has full stack manipulation facilities, so that you can do more than just sums. See the Manual for details.

## factor - Find the Factors of a Number

Here is another program for number buffs. This will any whole number and give you its prime factors - those prime numbers which when multiplied together make up the original number. Just type the command and the number:

**$ factor 24**
2 2 2 3

There seems to be no limit to the size of numbers that can be handled, though the larger they are the longer it takes. And did you know that the factors of 123456789 are 3, 3, 3607 and 3803?

## fortune - From Cookies

This is purely for fun, and may not be available on your system. Administrators have been known to close it off as users waste too much time with it. Try it anyway. Just type **fortune**. If it is accessible, it will print up the sort of message that you find in fortune cookies. These vary from the high-sounding but hollow:

Words are the voice of the heart

through the amusing:

System going down at 1:45 this afternoon for disk crashing

to the downright confusing:

)"%$#[[&!): missing '^' in asynchronous pipe indirection

If you can, write **fortune** into your '.login' to brighten the start of your day.

### sleep - Bide a While

With **sleep** you can build a timed delay into your system. This may be useful in a shell script to hold a screen long enough for people to read it. You can also use it in a multi-command line, running in the background, to produce a timed reminder. The command must be followed by the number of seconds. For example, this line will send a reminder message after 10 minutes:

   **$ (sleep 600 ; echo 'Time to Go') &**

### time - The Duration of a Process

Programmers may find this useful for testing the efficiency of alternative routines. A stopwatch is certainly no good for this, as the time a process takes to run depends upon the amount of traffic on the system as well as the complexity of the process.

Type **time** at the start of a command line, and when the process has finished, the system will report on how long it has taken:

```
$ time sort1 <testfile >sorted.out
real 6.5
user 1.3
sys  0.2
```

Three time values will be shown. These give the total elapsed time (real), the CPU processing time used by your process (user) and other active time - for disk-access and the like - in the system (sys). Some versions of **time** will also give the user/real fraction as a percentage, to show how much of the elapsed time the CPU spent working on your process. If you are the only active user, this will be close to 100%, but can drop to single figures at busy times.

## stty - Set Terminal Options

Treat this with care. The options control how your terminal interacts with you and with the rest of the system. Most of us should leave most of them well alone - they are there so that system administrators and other advanced users can a terminal to a new system, possibly via a modem connection.

To see the main settings, type **stty** by itself. For a full display, use the **All** option - **stty -a**. If that doesn't discourage you from messing about with the options, then nothing will!

```
$ stty -a
 -ignbrk  brkint  ignpar  -parmrk inpck    istrip   -inlcr   -igncr
 icrnl    -iuclc  ixon    -ixany  -ixoff
 opost    olcuc   onlcr   -ocrnl  -onocr   -onlret  -ofill   -ofdel

 nl0      cr0     tab0    bs0     vt0      ff0
 9600     cs8     -cstopb cread   -parenb  -parodd  -hupcl   -clocal
 isig     icanon  -xcase  echo    echoe    echok    echonl   -noflsh
 line=0
 intr=^c  quit=^| erase=^h        kill=^u  eof=^d   eol=^j
```

There are a few that we ordinary users may need to know about sometimes.

**echo** and **-echo** turn the on and off the echoing of keyboard input to the screen. This is not an option to set from the prompt. If you turn off the echo, you will not be able to see what you are doing when you want to turn it back on again. In a shell script, it will permit the discrete entry of a password - just remember to turn it back on again afterwards.

```
.....
echo Enter Password
stty -echo      { turn it off }
read pass
stty echo       { and back on }
```

The [Ctrl]-[Key] combinations that erase, end or abandon programs are listed in the bottom line of the **stty** display. These can be changed if you have learnt to use other keystrokes on other systems and would like to carry your working habits across. Give the option followed by the carat (^) and the chosen character. For example, to use [Ctrl]-[Z] in place of [Ctrl]-[D] as the End Of File marker:

**$ stty eof '^Z'**

One last and crucial option that you should know about is **sane**. If you have been fiddling with the settings so that the terminal is not in a happy state, type:

**$ stty sane**

This will restore normal functioning.

I can hear you asking how you can do this if the terminal is unusable. Don't worry, it can be done. There are two possible solutions. The crude, but generally effective approach is to turn the terminal off, wait a few seconds and turn it back. That should at least make it usable, even if not quite back to normal.

If that fails then try the second method. Remember that the terminal is a file, and that you can redirect any command to a file. Login at another terminal, run **ps -ef** to find out about your processes and get the filename of your locked terminal - it will be something like '/dev/tty16'. Now redirect sanity to that terminal's file:

**$ stty sane >/dev/tty16**

If that doesn't fix it either, then it's time to ask your system adminstirator for help.

# Chapter 16

# Shell Programming

What follows applies to the Bourne shell only. There are two main reasons why I have chosen to concentrate on this and ignore the C shell. The first is portability. Bourne shell programs will run in any Unix environment, though the inverse does not apply - you cannot run a C shell program where Bourne is the only shell. The second is space. There is scarcely room in this book to give a decent introduction to Bourne shell programming alone. It would be impossible to cover both adequately.

## Shell Scripts

In the jargon, a shell program is referred to as a 'script', to emphasise that it is a text file, and to distinguish it from compiled programs. At its simplest, a shell script consists of a set of commands, and when executed it has the same effect as if the commands had been given individually at the prompt. Such simple scripts are worth creating wherever you have a sequence of commands that you use regularly. Suppose, for example, that you always start the day by switching to your main working directory, listing its contents and finding out the date. A suitable script might read:

```
echo Good Morning
cd work
echo Switched to 'pwd' directory, containing:
lc
echo Today is
date
```

(Those are grave accents around `pwd`. See 'Command Substitution'. )

Use **vi** to write this into a file called 'start'.

We can run the script in three ways. You met two of these back in Chapter 6, but a quick reminder at this point may be useful.

## sh - A Shell within a Shell

**$ sh start**

This calls up a new invocation of the (Bourne) shell which reads the script and interprets the commands. After the last one has been performed, the system exits back to the original shell. For the most part, it is irrelevant that you are running a new shell to perform your script commands. It might matter if you were using variables, (see below), for these will normally only have any meaning in the shell in which they were created.

## The dot

Here we have a fine example of Unix' designers passion for brevity. The dot command (.) acts in much the same way as **sh**. The line:

**$ . start**

passes the 'start' script to the shell for execution. The main difference between this and **sh**, is that this doesn't set up a new shell. As a result, existing variables are accessible to scripts activated by the dot. A second difference is that you cannot pass parameters to your script if it is run this way.

## Executable Scripts

The third way to run a script is to make it executable. All this involves is changing the file's permissions. Files produced by **vi** - or any other text editor - will normally have the permissions set so that you have read/write access only. Give yourself execute permission with **chmod u+x**, and the script can then be run by simply typing its name:

**$ chmod u+x start**
**$ start**

If you want to test the examples given in the remainder of this chapter, you would probably find it simplest to create the script with a >redirected **cat**, if it is very short, and use **vi** only for longer scripts or for editing existing ones. Run them with **sh**, as it is scarcely worth making them executable if they are only going to be used once or twice.

## Variables in Scripts

Variables were introduced back in Chapter 10. You will remember that a variable can be called by more or less any name you like, and that a value can be assigned to a variable by an expression of the type:

**variable=value**

In practice, there's limited use in assigning values to variables at the prompt. Variables play a more important role in shell scripts, where they can hold data entered by the user and pass it on to other programs or use it to control conditional branching. The command to collect a string of data from the keyboard is **read**.

You can see **read** at work in this example script. It will collect the user's name and the day of the week, then echo back a cheery greeting.

```
echo Please enter your name:
read name
echo What day is it today?
read day
echo Hello $name Happy $day
```

Run it, and you should see something like this:

```
$ sh nameday
Please enter your name:
Bill
What day is it today?
Thursday
Hello Bill Happy Thursday
$
```

185

This is rather pointless, but - as you will see below - by combining variables with a simple branching structure, you can create shell scripts that will acts as menus to give easy access to a set of commands or programs.

Note that variables will normally only have meaning within the shell in which they are created, and that scripts run in their own shell. If you want to pass variables, or any changes to environmental variables, down to a script, they must be explicitly exported. The **export** only works one way, and does not allow you to pass variables back up to the previous shell.

You can test this by creating the two scripts shown below. The first sets up a variable 'name' and changes the PATH - adjust that line to suit your system. The variables are then exported and a second script is executed. This displays the contents of 'name' and PATH, then gets new values for them. It attempts to export them, but the values are not returned to the outer script.

```
{ call this vartest }
echo vartest script - testing export of variables
echo enter name
read name
PATH=~mac:~mac/examples:.:/bin
export PATH
export name
sh vartest2
echo Back to First Level
echo the path is now $PATH
echo the name is now $name
```

```
{ call this vartest2 }
echo vartest2 script
echo the name was $name
echo the path is $PATH
echo Enter new name
read name
PATH=~mac:/bin:/etc/.
export name PATH
```

Note that **export**, like most Unix commands, can take a list of parameters.

Sometimes it makes the script clearer to **export** each variable separately, sometimes brevity will be more important.

Run 'vartest' and you should get this:

```
$ sh vartest
vartest script - testing export of variables
enter name
Fred
echo vartest2 script
the name was Fred
the path is ~mac:~mac/examples:.:/bin
Enter new name
Suzy
Back to First Level
the path is now ~mac:~mac/examples:.:/bin
the name is now Fred
```

The PATH and name were exported successfully from vartest to vartest2, but the new values from there were not exported back. Edit 'vartest' to remove the **export** lines and run it again. You should find that 'vartest2' then has nothing for 'name' and displays the default PATH.

# Command line Parameters

Also called '**Positional Parameters**', these are a type of ready-made variable. When the shell scans a command line, any items written after the command are collected and stored in a set of variables numbered 1 to 9. These values can then be retrieved within the script by the expressions **$1, $2, $3** etc. To see this, create the following script, calling it **params**.

```
echo Parameter display
echo The first parameter was $1
echo The second was $2
echo The third was $3          { add more lines if you like }
```

Use **sh** to run the script, or make it executable with **chmod**. Don't try to run it with the dot command, as this cannot handle parameters. Whichever way you run it, type some words after the command.

187

**$ sh params one two**
The first parameter was one
The second was two
The third was                        { $3 is blank this time }

The shell command **shift** will move the parameter values along, so that $2 becomes $1, $3 becomes $2 and so on. The original $1 is lost in the process, of course. Edit your 'params' script to include **shift** as shown here, then run it again.

```
echo Parameter display with shifts
echo The first parameter was $1
shift
echo The second was $1
shift
echo The third was $1
```

Used in conjunction with some form of loop (see below), **shift** provides a convenient way to work through a set of parameters. If you need to know how many command line parameters were entered, the number is recorded and held in the shell parameter #. You may also like to note that the asterisk * is equivalent to the whole set of command line parameters. Test them with this short script, 'paranum':

```
echo Parameter Counter
echo You entered $# items
echo They were $*
```

When run, you should see something like this:

**$ sh paranum Tom Dick Harry**
Parameter Counter
You entered 4 items
They were Tom Dick Harry

## Comments in Scripts

#, the hash, has a second and completely different meaning to the shell. Written by itself - without the preceding $ - it marks the start of a comment. When the shell runs through the script, it ignores **#** and anything written after it on the same line.

There is an exception to this. In Berkeley version of Unix, you can force the system to run the script in a C shell by writing this as the very first line:

**#!/bin/csh**

The **#!** combination tell it to run the command, which is the C shell..

Comment lines can also be created by putting a colon (:) at the start. This needs to be treated with a little more care as the shell may try to interpret what follows the colon. To ensure that it is all ignored, enclose the comment in quotes. However you do them, comments are worthwhile.

```
: 'Comments make scripts more readable'
echo $thingy  # remind yourself what variables are used for
```

## Command Substitution

A command - whether it is a system utility, application program or another script - written into a script is normally executed as if entered at the prompt. The process that is running the script is put on hold while the command is managed by a new process, within its own shell. Any output from the command is displayed on screen or sent to a file, but is not directly available to the script. With command substitution, this output can be captured.

If you enclose a command in grave accents (`), then the shell runs that command and incorporates its output into the script. The resulting values can be passed to a variable or given to another command. In this script, for instance, command substitution is used to capture the current working directory in the variable 'start'. The directory is then changed, and a simple **pwd** is used to show that you are there. The 'start' value is later passed to **cd** to get you back to the original working directory.

```
start=`pwd`    # output captured
cd /
echo Working Directory is now
pwd            # output displayed only
cd $start
echo And we go back to `pwd` # output displayed by echo
```

You will find another example of this below, in **for ...** loops.

189

## test - Check Values and Files

In Unix, almost all condition testing is handled by **test**. This is a utility program, not part of the shell programming language - though as you can run programs from within shell scripts, the distinction is largely academic. It can check the status of files as well as test the values held by variables. If true, the exit status is zero.

The command is given in either of two forms:

**test *expression***     or     **[ *expression* ]**

If you use the second form, you must leave spaces inside the brackets. The nature of the *expression* depends upon what you are testing.

## test and Files

With files, there will be an initial option which defines the test. For example, **-f** will check that a file exists - as a plain file, not a directory.

```
$ test -f anyfile    { or [ -f anyfile ] }
$ echo $?            { exit status of last command }
```

This will echo '0' to the screen if there is a file called 'anyfile'. In practice, you would not use **test** as a stand-alone command. It is used in shell scripts and pipelines, where it can control the flow of events.

There are a number of other file-testing options, of which the following are probably the most important:

**-r** the file exists and you have read permission;
**-w** the file exists and you have write permission;
**-x** the file exists and you have execute permission;
**-d** the file exists and is a directory.

## test and Strings

String values are tested using the operators = and != (not equal), and the expression is accompanied, as always, either by the **test** word or enclosed in [ brackets ]. Take care with the punctuation. You must leave spaces

190

around the operator. Quotes are only necessary around the strings if they contain spaces or special characters.

**[ $password = letmein ]**     { true if they are the same }
**test $endflag != end**      { true if they are different }

If you just wanted to check that a variable or parameter held a value - without caring what it was - then all you need is the identifier.

**test $string**

## test and Numbers

Though command line parameters and variables are always strings, there are times when numerical testing is necessary. Some programs produce numeric values and all programs return an exit status to indicate success or failure. The operators here are abbreviations, rather than the symbols used in most other programming languages.

| -eq | equal | -ne | not equal |
|-----|-------|-----|-----------|
| -gt | greater than | -ge | greater or equal |
| -lt | less than | -le | less or equal |

**test $# -eq 4**  { true if there were 4 command line parameters }

## Compound Expressions

Any number of simple expressions can be linked together using the following operators, given here in order of precedence:

| ! | NOT | [ ! -d $file ] | true if file is NOT a directory |
|-----|-----|----------------|----------------------------------|
| -a | AND | [ -f $file -r $file ] | true if a file AND readable |
| -o | OR | [ $ans = y -o $ans = Y ] | true if ans is either y OR Y |

Where you are using a combination of NOT, AND or OR operators, operations can be enclosed in (round brackets) to force prior evaluation.

**[ ! ( $ans = q -o $ans = Q ) ]**

This will give a true value if 'ans' is neither 'q' nor 'Q'.

191

It is usually safer to use a series of simple tests rather than one complex expression. The shell can cope with either, but you will make fewer errors!

## Program Structure

Like all programming languages, the shell has a set of words that can control the flow. It is a very limited set, but it contains enough to let you repeat actions, and to make the performance of an action dependent upon certain conditions.

### if *test_is_true* then *action* fi

This is the simplest form of the **if** command. A value or file is tested, and an action performed if the test proves true. For example, to set up a cheery greeting to your favourite user, you could try this:

```
# iftest script
echo Who is that out there?
read name
if test  $name = Fred
then
    echo Nice to see you Freddy boy
fi
echo Bye for now $name
```

Run it, first with 'Fred' then with another name and you should see:

```
$ sh iftest              { or whatever you called it }
Who is that out there?
Fred
Nice to see you Freddy boy
Bye for now Fred
$ sh iftest
Who is that out there?
Jim
Bye for now Jim
```

This has only one action dependent upon the test, but there could be any number of commands between **then** and **fi**. These can be written one to a line, with no punctuation, or in a single line, punctuated by semi-colons. If you ran the commands at the prompt, the same rules would apply.

192

## if *test1* then *action1* elif *test2* then *action2* else *action3* fi

In a simple **if .. then ... fi** nothing special happens if the test proves false, and the flow moves on to the lines after the **fi**. If you want a false result to trigger an alternative action, then you need an **else** or **elif** (else if). This next example is my general purpose utility called 'do'. Feed it with a filename and then, depending upon the nature of the file, it will either change to a directory, run a program or pass it to the editor. The branching structure ensures that the actions are all mutually exclusive. The program only performs the actions after a 'then' if the preceding test is true, and having performed those actions, the flow leaps to 'Have a nice day'.

```
# the do script
if [ -d $1 ]      # is first parameter a directory?
then
    echo Changing to directory $1
    cd $1
elif [ -x $1 ]    # test for executable file
then
    echo Running program $1
    $1
elif [ -w $1 ]    # test for write access
then
    echo Editing $1
    vi $1
else              # not directory, executable or writeable
    echo What is this thing called $1
fi
echo Have a nice day
```

I suspect that the script needs some refinement if it is to be truly usable.

## Nested ifs...

The next script handles multiple branches using nested **if**s rather than an **if ... elif ...** structure. It is a front end to **vi** that creates backup files and ensures that a filename is given when **vi** is invoked. The outer **if .. else ..** branches on the test of whether or not a filename is given; the inner **if .. else ...** divides the flow for new and existing files.

```
# v - auto-backup for vi
if test  $1              # if a filename is given
then
    if [ -f $1 ]         # the file already exists
    then
            cp $1 $1.bak # create a backup file before editing
            vi $1
    else
            vi $1        # new file - go straight to vi
    fi
else
    echo Enter filename
    read file
    vi $file
fi
```

## while *test_is_true* do *actions* done
## until *test_is_false* do *actions* done

We'll take these two together, for the structure is essentially the same. Like **if**, they produce conditional execution of a set of actions, but with these, the flow continues to repeat for as long as a particular condition is (or is not) met.

At the simplest, the **while (until)** word is followed by a test, but there can be a whole list of commands before the **do**. It is the exit status of the last command in that list that determines whether or not the *actions* are performed. Test it out with these two scripts. The first **shift**s through a set of command line parameters, stopping when it runs out of values. Here the **test** follows immediately after the **while**, and the flow is identical to what you would see in a Pascal or C 'while' loop.

```
# whiletest script
while  test $1  # { true if $1 holds a value }
do
    echo Current parameter is $1
shift
done
echo The end of the line
```

Run it, with a few items in the command line:

```
$ sh whiletest a b c d
Current parameter a
Current parameter b
Current parameter c
Current parameter d
The end of the line
```

In the second example, the script keeps asking for a name and echoing a greeting until the word 'end' is entered. This time there is a list of commands between **until** and **do**, with the test being the last of them. It behaves like the Pascal 'repeat ... until' loop, or C's 'do ... while', but with one crucial difference. The actions after the **do** are conditional upon the test. In other programming languages a further branch command would be needed to achieve this.

```
# untiltest script
until
    echo Enter name
    read name
    test $name = end
do
    echo Hello $name
done
```

Run it and test it with a set of names:

```
$ sh untiltest { or whatever you called it }
Enter name
Fred
Hello Fred
Enter name
Sue
Hello Sue
Enter name
end                { notice that it skips the 'Hello .. ' line }
```

That last script could equally well have been written as a **while** loop, but the test would have to be negated.

```
while
    echo Enter name
    read name
    test $name != end      # { not equal to }
do
    echo Hello $name
done
```

The **do** action list is optional. Where you want a plain repeat-everything loop, the structure can be simplified to this shape:

```
until
    action
    action
    test
done
```

## case ... esac

The shell's **case** is functionally identical to C's 'case' and to the 'switch ... case .. ' in Pascal. It causes the program to branch in one of a range of directions, depending upon the value that is held by a given variable. This offers a far neater method of dealing with a range of values than using a long series of **if** statements or a complex **if .. elif ...** structure. Use it to set up a menu-driven script - one where there are a number of options and the user selects one by typing in a key word or character. The basic shape is:

```
case variable in
value1) action1 ;;     { single action ... }
value2) action2A       { or set of command lines }
        action2B
        ;;             { marks the end of an option }
value3)                { this generates no action }
esac
```

Note the punctuation carefully. There is a closing bracket after the value, and two semi-colons at the end of its related action(s). These are not needed on the last option before **esac**. The selector can be a single value or a set of alternative, separated by | bars. **x | X | q | Q** ) might all select Quit.

196

Such a shell menu is often the neatest way to control a linked set of file-handling programs. You could also use one to give a friendly front-end to your system. Create this script and try it out:

```
# menu demonstration
echo User-friendly Unix!
until                   # { to keep cycling back through the menu}

        echo List Directory .......... 1
        echo Change Directory ... 2
        echo Edit File ................. 3
        echo Remove File ........... 4
        echo Exit from Menu ....... 5
        read choice
        test $choice = 5
do
        case $choice in
                1) ls ;;
                2) echo Enter target directory
                        read dir
                        cd $dir
                        ;;
                3) echo Enter File Name
                        read file
                        vi $file
                        ;;
                4) echo Enter File Name
                        read file
                        rm $file
                        ;;
        q| Q| 5) echo Goodbye ;;     # alternative selectors
                *) echo Illegal Option   # { wildcard = any other choice }

        esac
    done
```

The * in the last line is a standard shell wildcard and can therefore stand for anything. It traps any values that are not handled by the earlier case lines. Miss it out and the script will crash if an unknown value is entered.

## for *variable* [ in *set* ] do *actions* done

In other programming languages, the 'for ... ' statement counts through a set of numbers, performing the enclosed actions each time through the loop. The shell **for** is similar with the crucial difference that it runs through a *set* of words. The 'words' are typically filenames, and the 'set' is typically a directory listing or the product of a wildcard expression. For example, the following would loop through a complete directory and send every readable file to the printer. (Don't run this unless you mean it and there's plenty of paper in the printer!)

```
# for demonstration script
for file in *
do
    if test -d $file
    then
        echo Directory: $file
    elif test -r $file
    then
        lp $file       # { cat $file would be safer! }
    fi
done
```

The 'set' does not have to be written into the script, but can come from the command line parameters. This next script, for example, will create a '.bak' copy of each file given in its command line.

```
# backcopy script
for file
do
    echo Copying $file to $file.bak
    cp $file $file.bak
done
```

Try it, feeding in a couple of files for which backup copies do not yet exist, then check the result by listing the '.bak' files.

**$ sh backcopy memo1712 update.pas sales92.rpt**
Copying memo1712 to memo1712.bak
Copying update.pas to update.pas.bak
Copying sales92.rpt to sales92.rpt.bak

```
$ ls *.bak
memo1712.bak
update.pas.bak
sales92.rpt.bak
```

## break and continue

These two shell commands provide ways of controlling the flow around **for**, **while** and **until** loops. With **break** you can leap out of a loop and back up to the previous level. **continue** allows you to jump the remaining looped lines and start the next repetition from the top. You can see them both at work in this example.

```
for file in 'ls'
do
    ls -l $file               # display each filename
    echo '(R)emove'           # offer choice of actions
    echo '(N)ext'
    echo '(Q)uit'
    read choice
    if [ $choice = q ]        # or we could have used case
    then
            break
    elif [ $choice = n ]
    then
            continue
    fi
    echo Really Remove?
    read ans
    if [ $ans = y -o $ans = Y ]
    then
            rm $file
    fi
done
```

Notice how command substitution is used to capture the directory listing in the first line of the script.

```
for file in 'ls'
```

The 'ls' is expanded by the shell to provide a complete set of filenames.

## exit [n]

**exit** closes down a script, and the shell that is running it. Give a number after the command to set your own exit status values. Miss it out and the exit status of the script will be that of the last command executed.

With more complex scripts, there may be several different reasons why they may fail. By marking each possible exit with a different value, the cause of failure can be identified.

```
....
if [ ! -f $name ]      # if name is not a file
then
    exit 2
elif [ ! -d $name ]    # if name not a directory
then
    exit 3
fi
...
```

# Number Values

The shell normally treats all values held in variables and parameters as strings of characters. This doesn't make number work impossible, but it does make it more difficult.

The **expr** utility program evaluates expressions in a variety of ways. What is important here is that it can convert a string of digits into a numerical value, and perform simple arithmetic with integers (whole numbers). Using **expr** we can pass numbers as parameters, count the iterations of a loop or even calculate.

As **expr** is a command program, the best way to get values from it into a script is by command substitution. For instance, to increment the value in a variable, we can use:

```
count='expr $count + 1'
```

If 'count' had held '4' before this, it would hold '5' afterwards. Note those quotes. They are there to remind you that the variables are always held as strings of characters. **expr** will evaluate the string, calculate and pass the new value back - but it will still be a string once it is back in the variable.

Watch the spaces! They are crucial. There are no spaces around the '=' sign, that assigns the value to the variable. There are spaces between the values and operators that make up the arguments to the **expr** command.

The arithmetic operators that can be used with **expr** are:

```
+ -     addition and subtraction
\*      multiplication
/ %     integer division    / = dividend    % = remainder
```

The backslash before the * is needed to prevent the shell from treating it as a wildcard.

The final two demonstration scripts look at simple uses of **expr**. The first will print multiple copies of a file. Named 'mprint', its command line would take the form 'mprint file number_of_copies'.

Within the script, the filename is the first parameter, $1, and the number is copied from $2 into the variable 'count'. This is used to control the repetitions of the **while** loop. It is tested at the top by the expression:

```
[ count -gt 0 ]
```

As the **-gt** performs a numeric comparison, nothing more is needed here to get the number value from the variable. At the end of the loop, the counter is decremented by the line:

```
count='expr $count -1'
```

You might also notice here the other two **test** expressions. At the top, the line

```
[ ! -f $1 ]
```

will produce a true value if a valid filename is not given. A few lines below, **if [ $2 ]** makes sure that there is a second parameter. It is not necessary to check that the parameter holds a valid number at this stage, as the **while** test handles that. Note that you will probably need to change the line that does the printing, to suit your system.

```
# multiple print utility
if [ ! -f $1  ]     # is the file present?
then
     echo Error - File $1 not found
     exit 1
fi
if [ $2 ]  # is there a count parameter?
then
     count='expr $2'   # count=$2 would work just as well
     while [ $count -gt 0 ]
     do
          lpr $1# or whatever command is used on your system
          count='expr $count - 1'
     done
     else
     echo Usage: mprint file count
 fi
```

This last script is really a bit of nonsense. There are far better languages than the shell for writing calculator programs, but it does demonstrate what you can do with numbers if you try. (It is also easier to use **bc**, the programmable calculator or even **dc**, which works in reverse Polish notation!)

Name this script 'calc', make it executable and you would use it with lines like:

**$ calc 2 + 3**

It should be self-explanatory apart from the treatment of multiplication. The asterisk is the multiplication operator, but it unfortunately has meaning beyond this. To make it work in the **expr** it is escaped by a backslash. As a selector in a **case** structure, it handles all unknown options, and rather than try and struggle to restrict its meaning, I have taken the easy route. If you want to multiply, then the sign is **x**.

```
# calculating in the shell

if [ $# -lt 3 ]
then
    echo Usage calc number sign number
    exit 1
else
    case $2 in
        +) ans=`expr $1 + $3`
        ;;
        -) ans=`expr $1 - $3`
        ;;
        x) ans=`expr $1 \* $3`
        ;;
        /) ans=`expr $1 / $3`
        ;;
        *) echo Unknown option
    esac
    echo $ans
fi
```

# Tips for Shell Programmers

**Try and keep it simple**. A script, like a Unix utility program, should do one job, but do it reliably. If more complex operations are needed, scripts can be linked in pipelines or called from within other scripts.

**Make it readable**. Use meaningful variable names and add comments wherever there may be any doubt about the effect of a line. Indent lines to bring out the structure. When you are debugging a script, it is much easier if you can glance down the side and see where loops start and end.

**Don't reinvent the wheel**. Before writing a new script, check the Reference Manual to see if there is something in that massive set of commands and utilities that will do the job.

**Test everything before you use it in earnest**. If you are processing files, run short test files through the script before you commit your real data to it. If you are writing a print utility, check the output on the screen before you risk the wrath of fellow users by clogging up the printer. If it is a file management script, that may remove files, test it when you know that a full backup has been done recently, so that files can be recovered if necessary.

**Watch your scripts at work**. Start up a new script with this:

```
$ sh -x script
```

The **-x** option will print out commands and their arguments as they are executed. You can then see exactly what your script is doing, as it does it.

# Appendix A

# Vi Command Summary

**vi** has two modes of operation: **Edit mode**, in which text can be moved, manipulated, deleted and corrected; **Write mode**, where the only edit facility is to rub out the characters that have just been written.

The commands fall into three sets:
    keystrokes in Edit mode;
    keystrokes in Write mode;
    **ed** commands in Edit mode.

These pages give a limited summary of the keystroke commands and a short list of the most useful **ed**-style commands. There are far, far more of the latter if you are interested. If, like me, you only use **vi** for programs and short text files and turn to a proper word-processor for the heavier stuff, then What is given here should be all you ever need.

# Keystroke Commands in Edit Mode

## Switch to Write mode:

| | |
|---|---|
| **a** | Add after cursor |
| **i** | Inserting before cursor |
| **o** | Opening a new line below |
| **A** | Add at end of line |
| **I** | Insert at start of line |
| **O** | Open a new line above |
| **R** | Replace from cursor (Overwrite) |

## Movement

| | |
|---|---|
| **h** or | Left one character |
| **j** or | Up a line |
| **k** or | Down a line |
| **l** or | Right one character |
| **w** | Right one word |
| **b** | Left one word |
| **0** | Start of line |
| **$** | End of line |
| **/string** | Go on to *string* |
| **?string** | Go back to *string* |
| **n** | Repeat last / or ? search |

## Editing

| | |
|---|---|
| **x** | Delete character under cursor |
| **X** | Delete character left of cursor |
| **dw** | Delete word |
| **dd** | Delete line - with copy to buffer |
| **yy** | Yank - copy line to buffer |
| **r** | Replace character under cursor |
| **~** | Change case  - upper to lower or vice versa |
| **p** | Paste line from buffer below cursor |
| **J** | Join current and next lines together |

## Repetition

. **(dot)**    Repeat last edit operation

All movement and Editing commands can be preceded by a number to give them multiple effect. e.g.

**3x**        Delete the next 3 characters
**6yy**       Yank 6 lines into the buffer
**4p**        Paste lines from the bufdfer 4 times

## Other - but Crucial

**u**         Undo the last edit operation
**ZZ**        Save and exit.

# ed-**style Commands**

In Edit mode, press [**:**] to access these. The cursor will appear at the bottom of the screen.

**:g/old/s//new/g** Search for old and replace with new throughout
**:q**              Quit
**:q!**             Abandon edit and quit
**:r** *name*       Read file into text at cursor
**:w** *name*       Write text to file *name*
**:n1,n2w** *name*  Write text from lines *n1* to *n2* to file *name*

# Keystroke Commands in Write Mode

**^H**        Delete character to left of cursor
**^W**        Delete word to left of cursor
**Esc**       Return to Edit mode

# Appendix B

# Quick Commands

This command summary is offered as a more user-friendly alternative to the Users Reference Manual and the on-line **man,** but a more limited one. The summary is highly selective. It concentrates on those commands - and on those options within commands - that are likely to be of use or interest to ordinary users. It does not aim to meet the needs of advanced users, shell programmers or system administrators.

Conventions Used:

  [item]     optional item - control letter, filename, string or number
  [item ..]   optional item may be repeated any number of times
  *item*      filename, text or number to be supplied by you
  filespec  one or more files, specified by a widlcard expression

Where no filenames are specified, input is from the standard input - keyboard, pipe or a redirected file; output is to the standard output - screen, pipe or a redirected file.

## banner

Creates large text for screen displays or printed headings.

    banner [string .. ]

See Page175

## cal

Gives a simple calendar for any month or year.

    cal [month] [year]

Note: As the year can be any value between 1 and 9999, it must be written in full.

See Page 176

## calendar

Scans a file called 'calendar' in the current directory and prints any messages linked to today's or tomorrow's dates.

    calendar

See Page 177

## cancel

Remove a file, identified by its request identification, from the print queue.

    cancel [print-id]

See Also **lp, lpstat**
See Page 41

## cat

Concatenates and prints files. Files can be joined together by >redirecting the output to a new file, or joined to the end of existing files by >>append-redirection.

cat [-s] [-t] [-v] [file ..]

### Options

-s   Suppresses 'File Not Found' error messages.
-t   Prints tabs as '^I', but only when used with -v option.
-v   Non-printing characters are displayed in the form '^X'.

See Page131

## cd

Changes Directory

cd [directory]

If no directory is given, the change is to the user's Home directory.

See Page 25

## chmod

Changes the permission mode of a file or directory. The permissions can be given in letters (symbolic) or octal numbers (absolute) modes.

### Symbolic Mode
chmod [ugoa] + - = [rwx] [file ..] { Symbolic Mode }

The first letter identifies the class of user:

| | | | |
|---|---|---|---|
| **u** | user/owner | **g** | other group members |
| **o** | any other user | **a** | all users |

The operator is one of:

+    add    -      remove    =      set the access modes.

The second letter identifies the access mode being changed:

**r**    read             **w**    write
**x**    execute (file) or search (directory)

## Absolute Mode

chmod value [file ..]           { Absolute Mode }

The value is a 3-digit octal number. Each digit is the sum of the permissions set for the user, in the order: owner, group, others.

Permissions are 'valued':     4 = Read    2 = Write    1 = Execute.

e.g.

chmod 750 file    =     chmod u=rwx,g=rx file

See Page73

---

## cmp

Compares two files, reporting the byte and line number at which differences are found.

cmp [-option ..] file1 file2

## Options

**-l**    Print the differing bytes as octal numbers.
**-s**    Suppress display of differences, and return exit status only.

The **exit status** is:

**0**     if the files are the same;
**1**     if they are different;
**2**     if a file cannot be found.

See Also **diff**
See Page 100

## cp

Copies files within or between directories. When copying a single file to a new directory, the original name can be retained or a new name given. Sets of files, selected by wildcard expressions, may be copied in bulk into a different directory.

    cp oldfile newfile
    cp oldfile directory[/newfile]
    cp fileset directory

See Also **mv**
See Page 55

## cpio

Copies selected files to and from an archive file, which may be on an external device (tape streamer or floppy disk).

    cpio -o[v]           { copy out to archive }
    cpio -i[dtv] [pattern ..]     { copy in from archive }

### Options
- **-o**  Outward copying to archive.
- **-i**  Inward copying from archive.
- **-d**  (with -i only) Directories are created as needed.
- **-t**  (with -i only) Creates a table of contents, without copying in.
- **-v**  (both -o and -i) Lists files as they pass through.

When copying out, source files are usually piped from **ls** or **find** and >redirected to the archive file. Original path-names are retained in full. When copying in, the archive file is <redirected in, and files recreated in the current directory, or in other directories as specified by their path-names. Files can be selected for copying by shell wildcard patterns.

**cpio** is far more comprehensive than this summary might suggest.

See Page170

## crypt

Encrypt or decrypt a text file, with encryption based on any chosen password. Files must be redirected <in and >out from **crypt**.

    crypt password [<clear_text] [>encrypted]
    crypt password [<encrypted] [>clear_text]

See Page 145

## csh

Invokes a new C shell within the existing shell, and executes a script if given.

    csh [-options] [script]

See Chapter 10

## csplit

Splits files into sets of lines, based on text items or line numbers. Each section ends on the line preceding the next text or number argument. The new filenames are made up of '**xx..**' , followed by a two digit number.

    csplit [-option ..]  filename [argument ..]

### Options
-**s**      Suppress the character count as files are created
-**k**      Keep files created so far if a bad argument stops the command
-**f** *base*  File names will start with *base* instead of **xx**

### Arguments
*/pattern/*      Write a file for the section up to *pattern*
*%pattern%*   Skip the section up to *pattern*
*number*      Section ends at line *number*-1

See Also **split**
See Page 139

## cut

Cuts selected fields from a data file, with fields specified either by field number or character position.

Input files are omitted when used in a pipeline;
output is to a >redirected file or the next command in the pipe.

```
cut -clist [file ..]              { character positions }
cut -flist [-option ..] [ file ..]{ field numbers }
```

### Options

**-c*list*** The *list* is a set of ranges, e.g. 3-10, separated by commas. If the start or end number is missing, then the start (end) of line is assumed.

**-f*list*** The *list* is a set of numbers, separated by commas, counting from 1 as the first field.

**-d*char*** Specifies the *char*acter to be used as the field delimiter, in place of the normal space.

**-s** Suppresses the output of lines with no delimiters. These might be headings for tables.

See Also **join, paste**
See Page 153

## date

Returns today's date and time. The superuser only may use this to reset the system clock.

```
date
```

See Page27

---

## dc

---

Desk calculator, working in reverse Polish notation. It is normally used interactively, but a command sequence can be passed in from a file.

dc [file]

**dc** recognises the operators:
+ - * / % (remainder) ^ (exponentiation) v (square root)

The key commands are:
**p**   print the value at the top of the stack;
**q**   quit

Additional stack manipulation commands are there if you are intereseted.

See Page 178

---

## diff

---

Compares two files and reports on their differences. The report is in the form of a set of lines showing the commands that would have to be given to **ed** to make the files identical. Unless you are into **ed**, the exit status is probably the most useful feature of this.

diff file1 file2

The **Exit status** is:
**0** if the files are identical;
**1** if they are different;
**2** indicates problems.

See Also **cmp**

## echo

Output text strings or variable contents to the screen. Intended for use within shell scripts, to prompt the user or to indicate the progress of the script.

echo [argument ..]

See Page 92

## egrep

Extended version of the **grep** command, that can handle more complex search expressions.

egrep [option ..] expression file

See Also **fgrep, grep**
See Page 129

## expr

Evaluate an expression. Mainly used for getting numerical values out of variables and performing calculations in shell scripts. All number work is in integers.

expr argument

An argument is a variable name alone or variables and/or values linked by an operator from the set:
+ (add) - (subtract) \* (multiply) / (division) % (remainder.

NB. The * must be escaped by a backslash.

In scripts, the command must be enclosed in 'grave accents' to obtain the resulting value.

See Page 200

## factor

Calculate the prime factors of a number.

>    factor [number ..]

See Page 179

## fgrep

Fast version of **grep**, which gains its speed by only handling fixed strings, without wildcards or other symbols.

>    fgrep [option ..] pattern .. file

See Also **egrep, grep**
See Page 129

## file

Take an educated guess at the nature of a file, or set of files specified by a wildcard expression.

>    file [ -f listfile ] file_specification

**Option**
**-f** *listfile* The files to be checked are specified in *listfile*.

See Page 115

## find

Searches through all the directories, below a given startpoint, for files that meet certain specifications. The search will typically be by name, type or time of last access or change. The names of found files can be output to the screen, a file or down a pipe. Files may also be passed directly to a command for copying, removal or other processing.

find pathname expression [action]

## Options

**-atime** *number* Files accessed since the *number* of days.

**-cpio** *device/file* Copies files to the *device* or *file*.

**-ctime** *number* Files changed since the *number* of days.

**-depth** Work upwards from the lowest directory.

**-exec** *command* Perform the *command*. Empty parentheses {} take the place of the filename in the *command*.

**-name** *filespec* Files of a given name or matching a wildcard pattern.

**-print** Causes the file names to be printed on the standard output.

**-type** *char* The *char* codes are **b** - block special; **c** - character special; **d** - directory; **f** - plain file; **p** - pipe.

The expression specification can be a single option and parameter, or several enclosed in brackets. The operators are ! (not) and -o (OR). AND is implied by the presence of two expressions. Brackets must be \escaped to get past the shell.

See Page 117

## grep

Searches through files for matches to a specified pattern, printing out any lines that contain matching text.

grep [options] pattern [files]

## Options

**-c** Only print a count of the number of matches.

**-f** *file* Take the search patterns from the *file*.

**-i** Ignore upper-lower case distinctions.

**-l** List the names of the files with matches.

**-n** Give the line number of each match.

**-s** Suppress error messages for missing files.

The files can be specified in the command line, or piped through from a previous command. The search patterns are a combination of straight text and symbols, of which the most important are:

.        standing for any character;
*       any number of repeated characters;
[*chars*] any one of the bracketed characters;
^       pattern at the start of a line;
$       pattern at the end of a line;

Patterns containing spaces or symbols, must be enclosed in quotes.

See Also **egrep, fgrep**
See Page 122

---

# join

Joins together the lines (records) from two datafiles that have a common field. The files must both be sorted into order on the common field. By default, this is the first in each line, and fields are separated by spaces, tab or newline. Each output line normally has the common field, then the remaining fields of the first file, followed by the remaining fields of the second file.

   join [options] file1 file2

## Options
   **-j***file_num field_num* Identifies an alternative field as the common field. Fields are counted from 1. If *file_num* is missing, the *field_num* applies to both files.
   **-o** *list* The *list* defines the fields to be output, with fields identified by number, in the form *file.field*, and separated by commas. e.g. 2.3, 1.4
   **-t***char* Sets *char* as the field separator.

See Also **cut, paste**
See Page 160

# kill

Closes down a process - especially useful with those that refuse to respond to less drastic measures. Unless the process is running in the background, you will have to kill it from another terminal. You will probably need to use **ps** to find the PID (Process IDentification number).

kill [-9] PID

The -9 option defines the signal number to be sent to kill the process. Though not essential, it does guarantee success.

See Also **ps**
See Page84

# ln

Creates a new symbolic link to an existing file, so that it can be accessed from another directory. The directory can be in another (user's) area on the same or a different file system. The linked file may be identified by the same or a different name.

When **rm** is used on a linked file, it only removes the link. This applies in the original directory as elsewhere. The file itself is only removed with the last link.

ln -s path/filename path/linkname

The **-s** identifies this as a symbolic link.

As linked files can cause problems when backing up, on some installations, the use of this command may be restricted to superuser.

See Page80

## lp

The main printing command, probably replaced in practice by a locally-written shell script that gives better control of the system's printers.

  lp [option ..] files

### Options
**-c** Make temporary copies of the files before printing. The files can then be deleted or edited without affecting the printout. The temporary files are removed by the system.
**-d***device* The *device* selects an alternative to the default printer.
**-n***number* Print that *number* of copies of each file in the list.
**-t***title* Print the *title* on the leading (banner) page.

See Also **cancel, lpstat**
See Page 39

## lpstat

Prints information about the status of line printer(s). Options specify the nature of the information to be given. Without options, it prints the current status of the user's print requests only.

  lpstat [option ..]

### Options
**-d** The default destination for **lp**
**-o***[list]* The status of output requests. The optional *list* specifies printers, request-ids or a mixture of both.
**-t** Total status information.

Other options cover specific aspects of the system's printers and print scheduler.

See Also **cancel, lp**
See Page40

# ls

Scans a directory and lists the names of files in it. Options control the layout and order of the list, the amount of additional information about the files, and the depth of the scan. If no path is given, the current directory is assumed; if no (wildcard) file specification is given, then all files - apart from those starting with . (dot) are shown.

    ls [-options] [path/][filespecification]

## Options
-**a**  All files, including those starting with . (dot).
-**C**  Column layout, with names sorted down the screen.
-**F**  Show filetype, marking directories with / and executable files with *.
-**l**  Long listing, showing permissions, ownership, size and date.
-**q**  Use ? in place of any non-printing characters in names.
-**r**  Reverse order of listing.
-**R**  Recursive listing, giving the contents of each sub-directory.
-**t**  List in time order, newest files first.
-**x**  Column layout, with names sorted across the screen.

See Page46

# mail

Read messages in your mailbox or send mail to others.

    mail [options]              { read mail }
    mail users [<message_file]     { send mail }

## Options

-**r**  Read mail in reverse order, oldest message first.
-**t**  When sending mail, this attaches to the message a list of all users who will receive copies.

When **reading mail**, use these keystroke commands:

+ -   Go to next or previous message;
d     Delete the current message;
s *file*   Save the current message as *file*;
*     Display a summary of commands;
q     Quit

When **sending mail**, either write the message directly after giving the command, ending with [Ctrl]-[D], or redirect an existing message file in the command line.

Your system may well have a more user-friendly alternative to **mail**.

See Page 76

## man

On-line help utility that prints entries from the User's Reference Manual.

    man command

See Page 65

## mkdir

Make a new directory.

    mkdir directory_name(s)

Directory names can be up to 14 characters long. The name may not include any spaces or the symbols:

   *.?:;!""'[]()\

See Page 52

## mesg

Open or close others' access to your terminal for messaging.

    mesg y    Open
    mesg n    Close

See Also **who, write**
See Page 94

## mv

Move a file, or set of files to a new directory, or rename a file.

    mv oldfile [path/]newfile   { to rename }
    mv filespec directory[newfile]   { to move [and rename] }

When being used to rename, **mv** can only work with one file at a time. If a file already exists with the *newfile* name, then it will be overwritten.

When moving, files can be moved in bulk using wildcard expressions, and retain their original names.

See Also **cp**
See Page60

## pack

Compresses a file or set of files. The originals are removed and replaced by the packed versions, marked by a **.z** suffix.

    pack [ -f ] filespecification

**Option**
**-f** Forces a file to be packed, whether or not it is worth the effort.

The packing process has overheads, and with small files these can outweigh the gains. **pack** does a before-and-after comparison and will normally abandon the attempt if it is not worth while.

Packing has most effect with simple text files. The smaller the range of characters, the greater the saving.

See Also **pcat, unpack**
See Page168

---

## passwd

Changes your password.

    passwd

For security reasons, **passwd** asks you to type your old password before allowing you to change it. If you have forgotten your old password, see your system administrator. The superuser can change any password without having to type in the current text.

See Page 29

---

## paste

Merges two or more files in columns. As a single tab separates one item from the next, columns will be irregular if the items vary in length.

    paste [-s] [-d*list*] file1 file2 ..

### Options

**-s** Use this option to **paste** a single - long, narrow - file into columns. If there are more than one file, they will be pasted into columns in sequence, rather than in parallel columns.

**-d***list* The *list* is the set of separators to be used in place of the normal tabs and newline, after the item from the last file. The characters in the list are used in sequence, cycling back to the start when they have all been used.

If one of the files is to be replaced by data piped from another command, indicate it with a dash (-) in the command line.

See Also **cut, join**
See Page 156

## pcat

The equivalent of **cat** for packed files.

    pcat file ..

    See Also **pack, unpack**
See Page 170

## pg

Displays a file, or the output from a pipe, a page (screenful) at a time.

    pg [option ..] [file]

### Options
| | |
|---|---|
| **-p** *string* | Set alternative prompt string. |
| **-c** | Clear the screen before each new page. |
| **-s** | Display messages in standout mode. |
| **+***line* | Start the display at *line* number. |
| **+/***pattern***/** | Start the display at the **grep**-style pattern. |

When **pg** is running, use these commands:

**[+/-]***num* **<CR>**   Move to page *num* or
move forward (+) or back (-) *num* pages.

| | |
|---|---|
| **[+/-]*num* l** | (Letter '1') As above, but counting in lines. |
| **[+/-]*num* d** | As above, but counting in half-pages. |
| **[*n*]/*pattern*/** | Display from the next line containing a match or the *n*th occurrence of a match. |
| **[*n*]?*pattern*?** | As above, searching backwards. |
| **s *name*** | Save the current file under the *name*. |
| **h** | Help. Display the commands. |
| **q** | Quit. |

See Page135

---

## ps

Reports the status of your current processes - or of any processes, if you are superuser.

    ps [-f]

### Options

**-f**  Gives full information about the process, rather than the normal user name, terminal, running time and command name.

See Page 84

---

## pwd

Displays the path to the working (current) directory.

    pwd

See Page 25

---

## rm

Permanently removes a file or set of files.

    rm [-options] filespecification

## Options

**-f** Forces removal without any check.

**-i** Interactive removal - each filename is presented for confirmation before removal.

**-r** Recursively deletes the contents of a directory then the directory itself.

See Page 58

---

## rmdir

Permanently removes a directory.

    rmdir directory

The directory must be emptied before it can be removed.

See Also **rm**
See Page 52

---

## sh

Invokes a new Bourne shell, within the current one, and executes a script if one is given. The start-up options given below may be useful when testing scripts.

    sh [-options] [script]

## Options

  **-e**   Exit from the shell if a command fails
  **-n**   Read commands but do not execute them
  **-v**   Display lines as they are read
  **-x**   Display commands and their arguments as they are processed

Other options are available. See the Manual.

See Chapters 9 and 16

# sleep

Does nothing for a given length of time. Mainly used for creating a pause in a shell script, or run in the background with an accompanying **echo** to give a timed reminder.

   sleep seconds

See Page 180

# sort

Sorts the lines (records) of a file into order on the basis of one or more key fields. The sort may be in ASCII, dictionary, month or numeric order. Can also merge - into order - two or more sorted files with the same record structure.

Unless otherwise specified, the sort takes the whole line as the 'key field'.

   sort [-option ..] [field ..] [file ..]

## Options

| | |
|---|---|
| **-c** | Check first to see if the file is already in the given order, and do nothing if it is. |
| **-m** | Merge two ready-sorted files. |
| **-u** | Output unique lines- do not repeat lines with the same keys. |

**-o***outfile* Send to *outfile* rather than the standard output.

| | |
|---|---|
| **-d** | Dictionary order |
| **-f** | Fold lower to upper case |
| **-M** | Month order |
| **-n** | Numeric order |
| **-r** | Reverse order - can be combined with any of the above |

**-t***char* Sets alternative *char* as the field separator.

## Key Field Specification

A sort may be based on several keys, and each key may extend across several adjacent fields. Fields are counted from 0 on the left. Keys are defined in the form **+start -end**, where *start* is the first field to include and *end* is the next field after the key. e.g. +2 -4 asks for fields 2 and 3 to be taken together as the key.

If an input file is to be replaced by data piped from another command, indicate it with a dash (-) in the command line.

See Page 149

---

## spell

Spell-checks text files against a resident word list, outputting a list of unrecognised words.

    spell [-option ..] file

### Options
**-b**   Use British, not US, spelling.
**+file**  Include your own list of specialised words, stored in *file*.

See Page 144

---

## split

Split a large file into sections, each of 1000 lines, or other length if specified. The new files will be named 'aa' through to 'zz', or will have those letters appended to a basename, if given.

    split [-num] file [basename]

**-num** Sets the size of each section in number of lines.

See Page 138

## stty

Sets the options for a terminal. Rarely required by the ordinary user, partly because the terminals may well have a simpler means of setting options built into their hardware, mainly because your system administrator should have set the terminals for optimum performance, and anything you do is likely to make things worse.

### Options
Many and various. See the Manual.

See Page 181

## tail

Display the last part - 10 lines by default - of a file.

    tail [option ..] file

### Options
**+/-*num*[lbc]** Sets the place from which to start the display, counting from the start (+) or end (-) of the file.
The count can be in **lines**, **characters** or **blocks**.

See Page 134

## tee

Makes a T-junction on a pipe so that output goes to a named file as well as to the standard output.

    tee [-a] filename

### Option
**-a** Append to the named file.

See Page 70

# test

Tests the value in a variable or the status of a file. The **test** command word can be replaced by **[ ]** around the expression, but the brackets must be separated from the expression by spaces.

The nature of the expression depends upon what is being tested.

## (1) File expressions:

    test -option file
    [ - option file ]

## Options
**-d**  Directory
**-f**  File, not directory
**-r**  Read permission
**-w**  Write permission
**-x**  Execute permission
**-s**  File size greater than 0

## (2) String expressions:

    test expression
    [ expression ]

### Valid Expressions

| | |
|---|---|
| **-z** *string* | String of 0 characters |
| **-n** *string* | String of 1 or more characters |
| *string1* = *string2* | Strings are the same |
| *string1* != *string2* | Strings are NOT the same |

## (3) Number expressions:

    test num1 -operator num2
    [ num1 -operator num2 ]

**Operators**

-**eq** equal
-**ne** not equal
-**gt** greater than
-**lt** less than
-**ge** greater or equal
-**le** less or equal

See Page 190

---

## time

---

Reports on the time it took for a command to execute, giving three values:
**real** total elapsed time;
**user** processor time
**sys** time elsewhere in the system;

time *command*

See Page 180

---

## umask

---

Sets the access modes for new files.

umask *nnn*

*nnn* is a 3-digit octal number that will be subtracted from 777 to give the permissions for a new file.

See also **chmod**
See Page 93

## unpack

Restores to normal a file packed by **pack**

    unpack file

See Also **pack, pcat**
See Page170

## wc

Counts the word, lines and characters in text files.

    wc [-options] file

### Options
-**l**    count lines
-**w**   count words
-**c**    count characters

See Page 143

## who

Shows the names, terminal ID and start time for those users who are currently logged on to the system. The special version **who am i** gives the name of the user logged on at the current terminal.

    who [-options]

### Options
-**H**  Print headings above the columns
-**q**  Quick version - gives only the names
-**T**  Also reports the terminal status. A **+** shows that the terminal is open for others to **write** to; **-** shows that it is not open.

See Also **mesg, write**
See Page 26

## write

Interactive messaging utility, copying input from your keyboard to another user's screen. The connection holds until [Ctrl]-[D] is entered.

**write** can only be used if the other user is open to receive messages.

write user

See Also **mesg, who**
See Page 78

# Index